PAULINE CROWLEY

Beyond Words

Edited by Karen Gardner and Anna McNay

VANWARD
PUBLISHING

VANWARD
PUBLISHING

VANWARD Publishing
Kent, UK

blurb

For Robert Christin

teacher and mentor
of the ALBRIGHT POETS

Acknowledgments

My mother and I are grateful for the generosity of those who shared their time in helping us to select and compile my mother Pauline's collection of writings. Several written pieces by her, which I had not seen before, made their way by post to my address in England when word got out that *Pauline Crowley: Beyond Words* was in formulation. A special thank you should go to Adela Kinne for recovering a number of her works following a minor fire.

A huge thank you to those who have helped with the editing and advance reading and reviewing processes: Anna McNay, Dr. Ed Winters, Mara Bergman, Denine Ellis, and Jemma Borg. It is with their critical analysis that we confidently forged ahead with the publication.

We are especially indebted to Pauline's close writing friends from the ALBRIGHT POETS: Linda Ardison, Marty Basden, Marilyn Broadhurst, Meredith Bunting, Nicole Entenza, Sandra Forte, Jeanette Gallagher, Barbara Dunn Hartin (died 2009), Jean M. Hendrickson, Kay Middleton, Maureen Mullin, Dorena Peterson, Sharon Poch, Jennifer Smith, Rae Spenser, Ann Tynes, and, most significantly, to Kathryn Brownlow who provided the history of the ALBRIGHT POETS. All these people played a most important role in the development of and continued interest in Pauline's writing. Their lasting friendship to my mother is cherished.

In addition, Jean Hurley, Pauline's sister, gives outstanding readings of Pauline's works when family gathers. Her strong voice is always appreciated. Most importantly, John, my father and Pauline's husband, has been part of this project every step of the way and his enduring dedication is an inspiration.

Karen Gardner

Foreword

To proffer a published book from a personal journal requires belief. I was confident when I asked my mother if she would allow me to go ahead with publishing her writings that their content would be read with a sense that they are universal, sharable, meritorious even, in nature. A book compiling the best of Pauline's work as a writer and storyteller will not only be a cherished treasure for family and close friends, but will also garner interest from the reading public.

Much of the development in Pauline's writing style can be attributed to the camaraderie of the circle of poets she spent time with, the Albright Poets. One of my mother's most respected writers in this group, Kathryn (Kay) Brownlow, offers a history of how they came to be formed:

In the late 1990s, Bob Christin offered a course on memoir writing at the Adult Learning Center in Virginia Beach, Virginia. A group of inexperienced strangers signed up and began to write. Thanks to the informal nature of the course and Bob's positive encouragement and feedback, they did not remain strangers for very long. Friendships formed and a core group continued to attend each new course he offered.

In 2000, under his direction, twelve of that group began to write poetry in its various forms. Over the next ten years the group met at Bob's house on Albright Avenue and dubbed itself "The Albright Poets."

At the same time, several members of that group were interested in continuing to write prose. Another informal group began to meet once a month under the direction of Pauline Crowley. Memoirs segued into essays and opinion pieces. Lunch with fine wine and lively discussions followed.

The dynamics of group criticism, suggestion, and evaluation have served to improve the quality of each person's writing. Several members have published books of poetry and individual poems in both online and print journals.

In 2011, Bob Christin moved to the Boston area, but a small group keeps The Albright Poets active. They still meet at regular times to share their work and offer critiques. Now led by Dorena Peterson, Pauline's group also continues to meet once a month to share writings and friendship.

My mother's struggle with bipolar illness, which is the subject of many of her writings, has intruded upon her productive life on several occasions as it has now. She has made up the deficit caused by this disease in the past and we wait with anticipation for Pauline to clear this hurdle again, to read and savour the wit and ludic usage of words in her new poems, memoirs and letters to the editor.

Karen Gardner

Contents

Reflecting Through a Train Window, Photo by Karen Gardner

Reflections

In a dark time, the eye begins to see
the occult sin of yesteryear.
With gloomy shade it comes alive
as lucid as the morning's sun.
But now in dusky and lurid glow
I fancy myself a fallen creature,
a one-time slave of passion and lust
who falls into the shadowy depth of despair.

Should I but wear the scarlet F
with outline somber and lacking sunshine?
Would I be able to put behind me
forever, the torment of a lost soul?
But could I more boldly, more simply,
more quietly imagine forgiveness,
I would see a glittering light
of redemption of my youthful self
and move from muffled shadows of the past
into the sanity and acceptance of a post-modern world.

March 12, 2007

Pauline Crowley

The Piano A SESTINA

Over the keys fly the fingers
Of the remarkable, talented woman.
And the mellifluous sound from the grand piano
Seems to lift the heavy depression
Of the townspeople at the open window.
So has the strength and magic of music.

The charm of the lively music
Encourages smudges from the dirty fingers
Of the townsmen on the window.
But not a bit cares the woman,
Who knows the effects of the depression,
As she gaily plays her grand piano.

Wealth is the hallmark of such a piano
Capable of such flawless music,
And the knowing, accurate depression
Of the keys by the bejewelled fingers
Of the generous, loving woman
Emit sweet sound out of the window.

She sits with her back to the open window
As she plays her grand piano.
The people are grateful to the woman
Who entertains them with such music.
And they play little games with their fingers
To prove they no longer have the depression.

It was the time of the solstice that the depression
Seemed to seep in through everyone's window.
And they could feel it in their toes and in their fingers.
And the closed, rosewood box that is the piano
Made no sound that resembled music.
For everyone, including the wealthy woman

Searched for ease. Even the woman
With her rings had the depression
And was averse to music.
But now in the spring she opens her window,
Sits down once again at her grand piano,
And plays it happily with fluttering fingers.

Time to banish depression, says the music.
And the woman sings as she plays the piano
For the people locking fingers as they stand at the window.

April 17, 2002

Post Mortem of a Saint IN IMITATION OF BARRY GOLDENSOHN

"Ye who travel, all ye who travel on the highway,
Hearken unto me, hearken and see
See if 'ere sorrow, was as my sorrow."

He lay in state,
The object of love and admiration
of millions who came from all over
the world. "There was no room at the inn."
Our Beloved Papa, leader of the faithful,
admired by all for humankind works,
but disobeyed in secret by the masses
who had come into the modern world.
I was among the latter,
skeptical, questioning, dubious -
"call me no more Naomi,
but from today call me Mara"
which means bitter, hypocrite,
sinner, unremorseful, infidel.
But still eager to attend the mass,
and receive the Eucharist,
my love and my tradition,
my companionship, my pastor,
my cradle to my grave,
the institute that binds me for life,
from the baptismal font
to the Columbarium
wherein is a slot for my ashes,
my name is on it.
Mara

April 25, 2005

The Convent School

Rigid rules
in my lifetime,
straight lines, narrow walls
enclosed me, affording protection
for and from me.
Stern voices, warning paeans
telling of punishment, of death
were my legacy.
All my life I have heeded,
and what have I missed?
Addiction, disease, unwanted children,
arrest, lawsuit, disaffection; but also
adventure, stretching, independence,
and perhaps – myself.

November 8, 2000

Class photo property of Pauline Crowley

She Walked on Air

When I was seven, I started taking catechism at the Catholic school in our parish. My sister Jean and I and one other girl from the public school met in a classroom there after the 8:00 mass on Sundays, where Sister Mary Paul Albert endeavored to teach us "Who made me?" and the response, "God Made me".

True to my innate form, I did not learn the lessons which were designed to prepare me for First Holy Communion. Sister talked to Mamma, and I was promptly transferred from the public school to the parochial school where it was hoped that total immersion in the religion would spark a learning interest in me.

There, all the children in the second grade were preparing for First Holy Communion: all the children, that is, except Betty Mae. Betty Mae had received her First Holy Communion the previous year. So every morning at the mass we attended before school, Betty Mae went to communion. She was such a pretty little thing – such a favorite of the teachers. If only I could be like Betty Mae.

"And remember, children," Sister Mary Paul Albert would caution us, "you cannot have anything to eat or to drink from midnight on, or you will break your fast and then you will not be able to receive your First Holy Communion."

I understood that warning and, on the Sunday morning that I was dressed in my white organdie dress and my net veil, I steered away from the kitchen and successfully made my First Holy Communion. The next day at mass, when Betty Mae went up to the altar rail to receive communion, I went too. After reception of the Eucharist, I blessed myself, folded my hands, lowered my eyes as I had seen Betty Mae do, and returned to my pew where I covered my face with my hands, again in imitation of Betty Mae.

"Pauline, aren't you going to eat your breakfast?" asked Sister Mary Paul Albert when we were seated in the classroom after mass. I looked at her. That's when I first noticed that Betty Mae was eating a brown bag breakfast. A gray shadow passed over Sister's face. "Did you have breakfast before you took communion?" She was incredulous.

It began to dawn on me that one must fast not only for First Holy Communion, but for second and subsequent holy communions. What a disaster! I could tell by the look on Sister's face that she believed that I was doomed to an awful afterlife punishment – and I believed it too. We took religion so seriously back then.

Betty Mae had a fine, clear, true singing voice. It was a real pleasure to hear her sing. Her mother held that she was singing before she talked. Because Betty Mae sang so well and had the lead in every performance at school, I persuaded Mamma to let me take singing lessons too. Betty Mae continued to have the leads, and I was consigned to minor roles, usually a maid. But I did not mind. I enjoyed listening to Betty Mae.

In eighth grade, the teacher-nun announced to the class who would have the lead in the end-of-school play. As usual it was Betty Mae. I personally took no particular notice, as far as I was aware, of the announcement, but, on the playground at recess, the nun called me and my good friend Pat Jackson aside, and she told us that she could tell by the look on our faces when she announced Betty Mae's lead in the play that we were jealous of her. Pat and I looked at each other. We could not believe what we were hearing. But we did not protest, at least not until the nun was out of earshot. Then we looked at each other in amazement that Sister had made such a wrongful assessment and we commented to each other about it.

That remark colored for a while my feelings for Betty Mae. Her piousness was more genuine than mine. Her voice was better. She was more talented. She was in our class, but not of our class. She was above the human feelings the nuns had for the rest of us. They treated her like some ethereal being dropped into their midst. Betty Mae had no close friends as the other children in the class did, no confidants. She was above and beyond us all.

We moved on to high school. Most of us girls went to a girls' academy, Betty Mae and Pat included. Betty Mae started taking singing lessons from a private tutor to develop her voice at that time, so the sisters at the academy did not take advantage of Betty Mae's prowess. They only used girls who took private lessons at the school in music and in drama to feature in their programs. Betty Mae went way into the background. Years later, she would confide in me that the sisters at the academy had treated her poorly except for the nun who was the librarian and editor of our Newsletter. When I mentioned that to Pat, she said sarcastically, "Well, she would say that because she was no longer teachers' pet!"

Last year I held a reunion for our class here in Virginia Beach. I rented a large cottage at Sandbridge Beach and assigned rooms to all the graduates of my class and their spouses who attended. Betty Mae elected to stay at a hotel on the strip instead of sharing a cottage which she felt would be primitive. When I told Pat that Betty Mae would be staying at a hotel, she remarked, "That figures!"

But Betty Mae is now a good, close friend of mine. She came to my mother's interment in Wichita where we had all lived and where Betty Mae and Pat and several others still reside. We had a good talk about the old days (the good and the bad) and Pat was not there to distract us. But Betty Mae remains aloof and other-worldly. She is the only one of us who has succeeded in getting all of her children (and she has five) to stay in the Church. She is truly blessed among us as she was so many years ago, standing on a pedestal with blue gown and a white veil, portraying the Virgin Mary, while the rest of us brought flowers to place at her feet.

November 28, 2001

The Fairest Flower

"Bring flowers of the fairest,
Bring flowers of the rarest,
From gardens and woodlands
and hillsides and dales."

St. Joseph's elementary school in Wichita, Kansas, was preparing for the annual Mothers' Day May procession. The little girls in first grade were learning to lead the procession slowly from the school to the outside grotto beside the priests' rectory. There, on a pedestal, stood a life-sized statue of the Virgin Mary. The lucky eighth grade girl who got to put the floral crown on Mary would have to ascend a flower-bedecked step ladder to reach her head.

I had been a part of this annual parade since I was a second grader, transferred from the public school where such lovely traditions did not exist. The second grade class followed the first graders. Two by two, girl with boy, we marched in the procession. It was too late for me to wish I were a first grade girl dressed in a long white dress with flowers adorning her hair, kissing rose petals carried in a basket before throwing them on the sidewalk to be trod on by the rest of the school. But I did long for the day when I would be chosen to wear the simple, long white garb and blue veil of the crowner of the Queen of the Mothers – the Queen of the May.

Such beauty I had never seen – such solemnity. However, as the boys approached the preteen ages, they were given to not being so malleable, and tended to clown a bit. Sister Mary Norberta came down hard on them, and they would try to get in line, but they were ungainly, clumsy, with feet and hands that looked like sculptures Michelangelo had exaggerated.

"Our hearts are all yearning,
Our glad voices turning.
For this is the loveliest time
of the year."

I never got tired of the annual May procession and I tried very hard to look pious so the sisters would pick me to crown Mary Queen of the May when I became an eighth grader. I was not the only one. All the girls aspired to the honor, and only one would be chosen – it was a lifetime event. No other chance would ever occur except when those of us who lived in large families got our younger siblings to do a May procession, and we ourselves crowned the little statue Mamma would keep on an occasional table. But it wasn't the same. No, being the crowner in the school procession was the ultimate in good, honest, pious living.

By the time I was twelve years old and in the seventh grade, I had a good chance to be the Queen Mary crowner the following year. I had an innocent look, devoid of carnal knowledge, my chest was flat, and my hair was abundant and long. The nuns liked me, and they commented on how good I was in a roomful of rambunctious youngsters. Actually, I was very shy, did not "get" jokes, and led a rather sedentary, quiet life – the sort I thought the mother of Jesus might have followed.

But the next year, I had to wonder what had happened to me. I exuded sex. My breasts were more fully developed than most of my girlfriends'; I appeared to be more the image of a Mary Magdalene than of Mary, the mother of Jesus. My lips had filled out, especially the lower lip, my brows were thick, and I had a glint in my green eyes. I towered over the majority of the girls in my class, as well as a majority of the boys. My skin had a rosy color. I was overlooked for the role of crowning the statue of Mary in the May procession.

Instead the nuns picked Rosemary Peak, a small, flat-chested girl with the pallor of alabaster and a puny body frame. I had tried to befriend Rosemary when she moved into our school three years earlier from Colorado, but she took offense and was actually mean towards me, deliberately stepping on my heels when I was in line in front of her. I never knew what about me offended her. But I felt, when she was selected to be the image of a Mary, that she certainly was not the mother of all nations.

"Oh Mary, we crown thee
With blossoms today.
Queen of the springtime
Queen of the May."

For the last time in my life, I solemnly marched in the May procession. Even though I would not be crowning the Queen of the May, the event had not lost its magic for me. I don't see many processions today, our church avoids them as if they were holdovers from immigrant days. But still in the Latin community the old Easter processions flourish and I feel that the people who so willingly take part in them, adults as well as children, benefit from the loosening of inhibitions to show their people and the world how deep their faith is.

Sunrise on the Elizabeth, Photo by Karen Gardner

An Epiphany

A dawn is arising,
A veritable truth of life.
I can see so clearly now
A spiritual epiphany awakening.
I can be holy without benefit of church,
Become alien to its pseudo spiritual
Belief in a virgin birth, in a resurrection,
in transubstantiation.
I can pray because I believe
It is beneficial to me.
Discard the preposterous postures
of kneeling, lifting,
Folding hands.
Atone for the church's past wrongs.
Be myself, no longer frightened of Hell,
Break free of the anguished circle
Of the church's language.

September 26, 2005

The Lecturer

Ladies and Gentlemen,
I come before you
to stand behind you,
and project these pictures
which I know nothing about.
The speaker will be my chauffeur,
Who remembers all that
I have forgotten.
Any questions should be
put in the box.
I will look them up
as the spirit moves me.
The next meeting will be held
At the round table of the
Four Square Gospel Church.
Now refreshments are held
in the restroom,
So let us thank the Father,
And the Son, and the Holy Ghost,
And race out of here to see
Who can eat the most.

September 14, 2001

Beloved Teacher

Sister Mary Genesius, B.V.M.
taught poor children on the west side of town.
Nothing was too good for us.
We viewed prints of "The Angelus,"
"The Potato Eaters," "Water Lilies."
We learned European history,
about Constantinople, the Crusades,
the French Revolution.
No one, not even the mildly retarded,
failed to learn to read at grade level.
We all worked fractions, decimals,
and diagrammed sentences.
Oh! the sentences we diagrammed.
Lucky me! I was privileged to
have been her pupil while
she could still remember names.
Years later, I was a stranger to her,
but no stranger to the knowledge
she had imparted.

July 11, 2001

Meadow, Photo by Karen Gardner

Mother, May I ?

The relationship between my mother and me is like homemade taffy. You pull it and pull it until it is shiny and pliant; then it forms a ribbon; finally a thread holds two parts together. The thread gets stretched until it breaks, then the two parts are put together to be pulled again.

I was like a filly that runs along free beside its mother as she pulls the cart or the plow, then they work in a double harness as the young horse matures. When I was eight years old, I folded diapers for my younger siblings to help Mamma with her chores. I stayed close to her really all of my life, learning from her, then doing things somewhat differently but still in the line of endeavor that she had followed, namely housewife – a negative term today.

I was able to take over for Mamma when I was a teenager and she had a menopausal depression. It never occurred to me to rebel – she was a good woman who had always been there for me, now I had to help her. I was in the harness until my sister married and new grandchildren revived my mother's spirits.

There were a brief two years when I was away from home for the first time teaching school. Living by myself in an apartment, paying my bills and figuring my income tax without my father to help me made me shaky, and my confidence in myself had not quite jelled; but there I was on my own as the nest was miles away. My father had helped me pack my car, then he said goodbye without a tear in his eye or a quaver in his voice. The tears, however, blinded me as I drove to Spring Hill to my teaching assignment.

I was back home in the summer after a two year stint at teaching. I was awaiting a reporting date to go to Lackland Air Force Base in Texas. Having had enough of teaching, I had enlisted in the Women's Air Force Corps. My father at that time was skewed. He wasn't himself. He had become addicted to gambling down at the Knights of Columbus hall and spent all night playing poker then coming home to get ready to go to work. My mother was upset. I was there for her. My father finally ruined his health with his obsessions and died a miserable death. I had never really needed much to become independent of him, but I did miss him and grieve for him. That was my time to comfort Mamma. I didn't have to advise her or tell her how to live her life as a widow though. Those concerns she worked out for herself uncomplainingly. She only needed me to be a part of her life.

"We are our mothers' daughters," writes Cokey Roberts in a popular book about the female gender and how we pass along learned values so we don't have to make old mistakes of former generations, but we are left free to learn new material after we have showered, shampooed, blow-dried, applied a bit of makeup, dressed carefully – a ritual we learned from our mothers, who learned it from their mothers.

"Are you and your mother the same person?" Dr. Beal, the psychiatrist, leaned across his desk toward me in earnest. I was recovering from a severe postpartum psychosis that had hospitalized me for three months of shock treatments and occupational therapy. My husband, John, had called my mother who had flown to Phoenix, where we lived, to take care of my children and the house until I could once again do it myself.

"We're somewhat alike, yet we're different somehow," I responded to Dr. Beal. He baited me with hints that my mother's bringing-up of me had been the cause of my insanity. I evaded him. I wanted to talk about concerns of the day, but he felt I would benefit in a group of people, who, as adults, were rebelling against their mothers so that they themselves could reach fulfillment as independent individuals.

I was shocked by what I heard – grown people writing their mothers awful letters of condemnation, of wailing about their dysfunctions caused perhaps by their toilet training. One man my age (which at the time was thirty-three) had been reared by his aunt who had stepped in to care for him when his mother died at his birth. "My dear, dear boy," she would write. He would angrily reply with "I am not your dear boy," then go on to lambast the poor, unknowing woman.

I refused to get caught up in that activity. I knew my mother had not been responsible for my mental problem. And didn't I need her there to help me until I could take control again? She would never understand such railings; she would be hurt, confused. I looked askance at my three little children. Would they grow up to accuse me so unjustly of problems they were sure to face? I vowed I would remember to keep it light. Too serious a demeanor brings only agony to everybody.

Now Mamma at the age of ninety-four lives with John and me. She has been here two years. She is easy to live with. I only do for her what she cannot do herself – put on the meals and pull on her support hose. She spends her days and her nights in her own room reading, writing, reconciling her checking account, watching television. She does not impinge upon my life. She never complains and neither do I. I enjoy having her here.

Last week she and I went out to lunch with a friend. To get her back into the house, I had to help her put one foot on each step then I gently pushed her from the behind while she pulled herself up with her arms.

"You're good at that, Pauline," my friend remarked.

"I had a good teacher," I replied.

I guess I'll never really be my own person as Dr Beal wanted me to be; but he was a visionary with ideals that I did not buy. And why not be like Mamma? She has made an emotional, spiritual, and financial success in her life. She has eighteen grandchildren, each individual one of them thinking that he or she is her special one. She has great-grandchildren who write to her, who bring her homemade goodies. I can only hope to duplicate her good life.

September 27, 2000

Pauline Crowley

The Couplet A PANTOUM

The couplet is two equal lines
Lines that tell a story
Create a vignette for the reader
The loves or adventures of a hero

Lines that tell a story
To embellish, enrich our lives
The loves or adventures of a hero
Carry us to different places

To embellish and enrich our lives
Though we may not leave our home
Carry us to different places
These are found in prose and poem

Though we may not leave our home
We have the capacity for experience
These are found in prose and poem
Others' lives are at our beckon

We have the capacity for experience
Experience that eludes us every day
Others' lives are at our beckon
And in a couplet life is reborn

In Shakespeare, Chaucer, and also Frost
The loves or adventures of a hero
Are related on paper to thus transport us, as
The couplet is two equal lines

Favor or Fear

I used to buy the notion wholesale.
The idea of an afterlife.
Perhaps the given that we may lose our conscious,
the thing that thinks, that remembers, that anticipates,
was too much for some to bear.
So the concept of life after death
became a metaphor for enjoying ad nauseam
a celestial home where one enters
through pearly gates, St. Peter taking roll,
harps playing, angels singing.
It sounds as boring as an afternoon
on the beach with nary a book to read.

On the other hand there is Hell, a place
of much distress and burning,
a revenge for your enemies
forgetting you are someone else's enemy.
I believed all my youth that my
indiscretions with Hugh Cotton under
the Spirea bushes condemned me eternally.
Oh, the eschatology of it all.

Today I think my life after death
will be my body giving sustenance to worms, to plants,
to the atmosphere those still living breathe,
and my mind will finally be at rest.

Empty Purses

Empty purses, empty purses
And they all belong to the unemployed
The retired, the marginal, the poor.
And it's all due to derivatives,
Collateralized debt loans, bundles,
Securitizations, foggy toxic assets.
The greedy barons of Wall Street
Robbing the denizens of Main Street.

Empty purses, empty pockets
Jobs are lost, insurance is lost, homes lost.
But things are turning around
Not a revolution, but evolution
Which is as slow as convolution,
And the same people come out on top
With pay raises, bonuses, and stock options.
They have so little touch with the faces
Which beg at charities, eat at soup kitchens.

Come. Let's turn this economy on its head,
Distribute more evenly the goods of earth,
Be satisfied with a full plate
Instead of gobbling up the whole.
Then our ways of life would return
To a more equitable, accountable society
That counteracted the growing number
Of homeless, of hungry, of disadvantaged.

(757) 446-2051
via e-mail: letters@pilotonline.com

Providing for others

In "Regaining responsibility" (letter, March 14), Caleb Carroll wrote about the benefits of giving an individual full authority over his money instead of having a Social Security system that collects through the working years, then doles out in retirement — a system a person can depend on.

This seems to be a sinister scheme that would engender a certain *Schadenfreude* of "I made it, and you did not."

I have no problem with living like a Republican — conservative, frugal, attentive to investments. But I always vote the Democratic ticket to try to provide for those who do not have my expertise, my skill and, most especially, my sheer good luck.

Pauline Crowley
Virginia Beach

Virginian-Pilot, March 19, 2004

Pauline Crowley

Integrity

It was out on the prairie where the sun shines hot,
Edith Wagner had planted her garden plot.
But when she used the hose to give it a spray,
Dave, her husband, took it away, saying
The trees which are permanent tenants of the land
Need all the scarce water they have on hand. Later
she stood at the dinette window overlooking her
plot, the radishes, cucumbers, lettuce and
tomatoes going to rot. Next week's salad
wilting away. Yet, why could she say? What
could she say? And a few tears slid down her
puffy cheeks by her nose as if to give moisture
to the plants in their cultivated rows.

And Tom, the hired hand, who sat at the
table finishing dinner felt his heart lurch
for the boss's wife. (Though he was never
before lustful in his life.) He desired to
caress her, to hold her close, to kiss her,
to suck her, to give her a hug,
to roll around with her on the rug,
to take her finally standing up.
But he finished his coffee and put down
his cup. He got up from his chair and
went outdoors.
It was time for him to finish his chores.

March 6, 2002

The 'Write' Stuff

My maternal grandmother died when my mother was but eight years old. She was the oldest of three children; the two younger ones were boys. My grandfather needed a woman on his farm, and eligible women were in short supply there on the Oklahoma prairie. So he advertised for a wife in the New York paper. I have never been privy to the contents of that request for a woman, but I am in possession of a letter from the brother of a young widow who answered that cry in the wilderness. He wrote to my grandfather the following:

Dec. 7, 1915

Dear Sir,

My sister, Mrs. E. Simmons, has made me acquainted with the fact of her correspondence with you. Also, she has read to me your letters. While I am not opposed to such a method of forming acquaintance, I realize that great care must be observed on both sides regarding compatibility of temperament, honesty of purpose, and general characteristics of honesty, culture, and morality.

My sister is a woman of fine perceptions and of an intense morality which abhors and cannot possibly tolerate coarseness of mind or speech in others.

Such was the tone of the written word back in the early 1900s. My grandfather was duly impressed, and so this scrupulous Edith came to join the family as stepmother to my mother and her little brothers. Immediately, there was installed in the family schedule time for reading and writing. By the lamplight in the evenings Edith would read Jack London stories to the family, and even little Davie sat quietly and listened.

She encouraged the children to write letters to relatives and friends, and, as the editor of her former husband's women's magazine, she corrected their grammar and their punctuation. Among the many items she brought from New York was a cardboard box full of stories hopeful writers had submitted to the magazine for publication. Those were stored in the hayloft of the barn, and, when Mamma had some free time, she would climb up there and read the handwritten stories. Then she would try to fashion stories of her own.

This stepmother of my mother was known to me as Grandmother, and she extended to me the same encouragement to read and write as she had to her stepchildren. I looked forward to Christmas because I could hardly wait for the book Grandmother would inevitably send me. Then I and my brother and sister would devour its contents. "The Wizard of Oz", "The Five Little Peppers and How They Grew," "A Child's Garden of Verses," "360 Bedtime Stories," and "Tales of Shakespeare" by Charles and Mary Lamb were just a few of the books she sent us. I owe my love of good literature to her as well as the enjoyment I get from sitting down and writing.

When I was twelve, I spent the summer back on the family farm. I had an experience with a horse and a barbed wire fence that got enough attention to make the local paper. My grandmother mailed me a cufflink that had been her first husband's. It was faux gold and had a horse embossed on it. The front legs of the horse were stretched out into a gallop while the hind legs gathered momentum. "This is the way the horse was going when it threw you into the barbed wire," wrote Grandmother. "Why don't you write about your experience?"

After much thought and recall, I penned the following story: *"An Ill-fated Horseback Ride"*

I still loved going to the country. Our visits to the family farm were all too short and infrequent. I longed for a summer's stay at my uncle's farm.

Uncle George's wife Genevieve did not care to have me for any length of time, but Uncle Dave's new wife was very hospitable and told my mother she would be happy to have me for an indefinite stay in the summer of '42.

So I packed a box lovingly, including my new jodphurs which I had found at the dime store and which I had begged Mamma to buy for me. Mamma got a bus ticket and saw me off for a glorious stay on the farm.

First day there I put on a blouse and my new jodphurs, ran out of the house, called Poochie the dog to accompany me; and I made my way to the barn. There stood Uncle Dave's new horse, Buck, all bridled and saddled and waiting to give me a ride. I went to put my foot in the stirrup to leap into the saddle. But! I could not bend my knee. The jodhpurs were too tight. No wonder English riders had lackeys to boost them onto their horses.

"Do you want me to lift you up?" asked the hired man after he had had a good laugh at my predicament.

No, I did not want to be lifted on. I went back to the house and changed into my skirt which I would be wearing for the rest of my stay. Then I had a pretty good ride – but Buck was well-named.

The days droned on, and I was happy. But the prairie was

plagued by a drought that year, and the parched land grew dusty, but not as bad as in former years. The mood of the grown-ups was solemn.

One day I was in the yard playing when I noticed the milk cows were all congregated around the stock tank. They were bowing and moving restlessly. The stock tank was almost dry, and what water that was in it they could not reach. I hated to see them suffering so.

I went into the well house that was adjacent to the stock tank and I checked the water in the barrel. It seems the windmill pumped water into that barrel and then it ran down a pipe to the stock tank. The barrel was not brimming, but the water was high enough to get some out for the cows. So I took the wash basin that hung in the well house and dipped it into the water. Did it make the water recede too much? I did not want to deprive the household of its needs. No, the water came back up to the same level it had been before I removed some. The pump was working weakly.

I took the basin of water over to the barbed wire fence and pushed it over to the other side where the suffering cows stood. The lead cow, Bossy, came to slurp it up. Then I got another basin of water, and after driving Bossy off gave another cow a drink.

One by one every cow got a basin of water, and even though it was just a small draught for their needs, I felt they must be more comfortable.

Then I decided to have myself a little ride. I went to the corral where Buck snorted and stomped. He did not want to have the bit in his mouth or to give me a ride. I did him the favor of leaving the hot saddle off, led him out of the corral, and got him close to the rail fence where I could mount him.

We took off across the road to the stubble field beyond, and I kicked him into a canter. He went into a frenzy and took off like a race horse. I tried to rein him in, but he wanted his freedom. He headed back across the road and raced toward the barbed wire fence. My skirt ballooned out behind me, and I hung on for dear life. I thought he was going to jump the fence or run into it, but he stopped short and sidestepped the fence. I did not stop. I slid off him sideways and felt a sharp sting on my buttocks. The barbs on the fence had done a number on my tushie.

The hired man and woman rushed me into town where the old country doctor clamped my cuts together and gave me a tetanus shot. I felt abused. I had done a good deed for animals that afternoon, and it was an animal that had done me a mean turn.

I cannot say Grandmother's encouragement made me into a someone, but like the embroidery and sewing I learned at my mother's knee and the game canniness I learned from my father, skills that have lasted a lifetime are not only a joy to perform but are also a therapy to be practiced all my life through.

October 4, 2000

Photo property of Pauline Crowley

And Now We are Five

In 1938 when I was eight years old, my mother called me aside to have a little talk with me. "Pauline," she confided, "I am going to have a baby. You are a big girl now, and you must help me more. Your new job will be to bring the clothes in off the line."

I was amazed. Mamma was going to have a baby. But how? That she did not tell me, but she did explain that the baby would be growing in her abdomen, and I was to watch her get bigger.

Oh joy! A new baby in the house. Ruthie was already three years old and did not like to be picked up by me anymore. Thrills of anticipation trilled up and down my spine. I would be the envy of the Protestant girls in the neighborhood who were only children. They had never had the privilege of having a warm, snuggly baby in their houses.

Actually, I put it out of my mind, as I was preparing for a Christmas program at school. I was having a difficult time learning the words of the song we third graders were to sing and the dance steps that went with it. We were to be Chinese peasants singing, "Planting rice is no fun."

"Pauline," Sister Mary Paul Albert was calling my name, "please take this note up to the principal's office."

How important I felt delivering a message. I climbed the stairs to the second floor, where the principal taught the eighth grade class, and I knocked on the door. Sister herself answered it. I handed her the note, and she opened it and read it.

"All right, Pauline, go back to class," she directed.

When the dismissal bell rang, I went to the cloak room to get my jacket and my leggings. A sissy boy not many children liked came up to me and spat out, "Sister told us you are poor."

I couldn't move. I had been betrayed by a nun I had liked and trusted. She had sent me out of the room so she could disclose to my classmates that I was poor. (Of course, she may have meant I was poor in spirit – the church talked a lot about those so inflicted then.) But to my little mind, she equated me with Betty Zenner who lived in a Hooversville slum outside of the city and whose clothes were thread-bare, whose hair was unkempt. My mother was an excellent seamstress and she made her children attractive clothes. She washed our hair and curled the girls' hair. And we lived in a nice little bungalow in the city. Of course, there was a depression, and... and... – well, for goodness sakes, weren't we all poor in those days?

I could hardly put one foot in front of the other as I walked home. Why was Mamma going to have a baby anyway? Resources were pinched. Jean, who was nine, was complaining she didn't have any pennies to play bingo, and I was yearning for a cent to buy a licorice stick or a jawbreaker. We were already six people crowded into our two-bedroom house. It just didn't seem decent to bring another soul into our little world.

I burst into the house ready to rail at Mamma, but Daddy met me at the door. What was he doing home at this time? Had he lost his job again?

"Mamma had her baby. She's at the hospital, and she wants you to visit her."

I gave a whoop, and my recently paralyzed legs took flight. I soon arrived at the hospital and found my mother's room. Oh, she looked so warm and comfortable and stable lying there in the bed with numerous pillows propping her up. She was looking over a menu.

"Come here, Pauline, and see how I select what I want for dinner tonight."

I looked at the card. She had checked chicken noodle soup – a family favorite.

"Go down to the nursery and see your baby brother Joe," she said.

So the baby was a boy, and his name was Joe. I went down the corridor to the wide-windowed nursery and saw numerous newborns wrapped tightly in their bassinets.

There he was, Joseph Dobrott. He was so sweet. Such a long, thin neck and full lower lip. He was so cute. I could hardly wait for him and Mamma to come home so I could sit in the rocking chair and hold him close. My mean, unholy thoughts completely disappeared.

Now we were five, and five we would remain. Jean, Pauline, Bobby, Ruthie, and Joe. It sounded like a song. Jean, Pauline, Bobby, Ruthie, and Joe.

September 29, 1999

Pauline Crowley

The Cloud of Imagination

Every night as my grandfather sat
And read to us children stories from
Zane Grey, from Arabian Nights, from
Hans Christian Anderson,
We sat enthralled, Jean, Joe, Bob
Ruthie, and I
Floating on a cloud of imagination,
Of words and phrases and whole
Convoluted sentences.
So began our love affair with books,
With tales of courage,
Adventure, love, and mystery.
I can still see the old fellow –
His face wizened with age,
His head hoary, and rimless
Glasses enlarging for him the
Print; although he knew the
Stories by heart.
And my heart aches to once
More sit beside that dear
Old man and travel away
In fancy and imagination.

Who is Mrs. Dover?

My mother, shy and rural-minded, was hard put to fit in when we moved to the big city of Wichita, Kansas, when I was four. We lived in a neighborhood of small bungalows, but on the corner to our right was a large, two-storey house occupied by an indigent family from Arkansas. The parents had five children, but three were already gone from the nest leaving a twelve year old girl, Lois, and a four-year old girl, Clara. Their surname was Dover, and the mother was forever after known to us Dobrotts as Mrs. Dover – never her first name.

Once I was in the big house they occupied. It was strewn with old, ragged clothes everywhere – on the table, on the chairs, on the staircase. The exception was a lovely bridal gown hanging from a door, as if a Cinderella lived on the premises. But that royalty was not Mrs. Dover. Mrs. Dover was gone to pot, her body heavy and slovenly, her hair unkempt, her shoes run down. She was the epitome of what I felt disgust for. Occasionally her husband, who was a truck driver, would come home and beat her. One evening she ran down the street yelling "Help! Help!" with her husband hard behind her with an ax. We couldn't call the police. We did not have a telephone. This was the woman Mamma befriended.

When my fifth birthday approached, Mamma told me that she would give me a party. I was elated, excited – that is, until she told me that Clara Dover would be five the same day and she would be feted too. My mouth fell, my throat went too dry to protest. But I was disturbed enough to ruin the party for Clara, for myself, for Mamma, and for everyone else. Mamma never had another party for me.

We moved. The Dovers moved. We were still within walking distance of each other, and often when I came home from school I would find Mrs. Dover sitting at our kitchen table having a cup of tea with Mamma just when I wanted to share my day with her. I would put on a surly face.

"Say 'hello' to Mrs. Dover," my mother would command, so, with no friendliness in my voice, I would say "hello." Often Mamma was reading and interpreting a letter from Social Services to Mrs. Dover, as the woman was illiterate. By that time she was divorced and had only Clara at home as Lois had completed high school and had married. Mrs. Dover and Clara were on welfare. I myself had reached teenage and was clever at pin curling hair. I often did Mamma's hair for her as she never got the knack for pin curling. Occasionally she would shampoo Mrs. Dover's hair at the kitchen sink then ask me or my sister Jean to pin curl it. How I hated to touch that woman! She was so beneath us, so subservient, but she always had a smile for me as if hoping I would mellow my feelings for her a little. She was respectful, perhaps a little too ingratiating, but she never let my hostility for her interfere with her friendship with Mamma.

One day I was down in the basement washing clothes and running them through the wringer when Clara Dover came crashing down, her mother hard behind her trying to punish her for something (I knew not what), although she was beyond the age of being reached by punishment. Clara let go of a profuse string of profanities, probably learned from her father, and I saw how helpless Mrs. Dover was with her youngest child. There was no esteem in that family – they were the poor of the poor, whereas I was the *rich* little poor girl.

When I married at age twenty-eight, my mother had Mrs. Dover come sit in the house with the gifts while we were at the church and reception. By that time I was glowing with happiness for myself and everyone else, and I let Mrs. Dover know how I appreciated her presence. She smiled a genuine smile.

The next decade went by very slowly for me. I was adjusting to living with a man now my husband and wondering when the children would stop coming. I was so fatigued I went through my days like a zombie. One morning I felt particularly ill with a symptom I could not then and cannot now describe. I prevailed upon a neighbor friend to watch the children while I went to the doctor. I used a clinic composed of several doctors where appointments were not needed. The patient went in, signed a register, then sat down and waited until he or she was called. I signed in and sat wearily down. In no time at all I had fallen into a deep sleep. Forty-five minutes later I awakened and my symptoms were gone. I scratched my name off the list of patients still waiting, and I went home refreshed. I had only needed rest.

John was on the fast track at work and he was only present to me to complain about something or to have me smiling on his arm at an office function. On those occasions I cringed at my miserable wardrobe. It seemed I never had anything appropriate to wear. I just did not have time or energy for shopping. I put on weight and did not get much exercise. Time was slipping by, the children were in junior high, and I felt like I was a dysfunctional mother. How had I gone from an attractive career girl to this position?

One day on the first of February I awakened to a case of the flu. I drove three blocks to the 7-11 to get an over-the-counter medication and a police car followed me home. The policeman got out of his car as I got out of mine and he told me that I did not have an up-to-date city sticker on my car. I was in violation of the law. He filled out a ticket for me asking me what my occupation was.

"Nothing," I answered. "Put that down – nothing," I demanded. He wrote "housewife" in the blank. Same thing, I thought.

Karen, our daughter, was thirteen and she wanted a Social Security card. Legitimate request, I thought, and I drove her to the Social Security office in Norfolk. When we emerged from the car, I heard a long whistle, whee-whoo. I looked to see where it had come from and a workman yelled, "Not you! The girl!" How dare he? I pushed Karen behind me to shield her from the lascivious eyes. That's when I saw her – Mrs. Dover coming out of the Social Security office. What was she doing here? Could I be mistaken? No, it was the same sloppy broom stick skirt, the run-down shoes, and besides, I saw a glimpse of recognition in her eyes. I waved at her as she waved at me. Then I gasped! This was not Mrs. Dover – it was I, I, reflected in the opaque glass door of the building. I had become Mrs. Dover. All my appreciation of fine things had evaporated in the space and time of my quasi-misery.

Today I realize that there are millions of Mrs. Dovers in the country, some poor, some uneducated, some abused by husbands and children, some just messy, some with a combination of the attributes that steal away a woman's esteem and self-worth, her creativity.

January 9, 2002

Books

I think that I shall never look

at something better than a book.

A book whose words comprise a tome

of scenes that make you feel at home

with romance, mystery, sports, and law

and lives you live with utter awe.

Words that transport you to fancy flight.

Oh God! What a rare delight!

Pies are made by housewife cooks,

But clever authors write good books.

There is no frigate like a book
To take us lands away,
Nor any coursers like a page
Of prancing poetry.

Emily Dickinson

The Frigate

Tears were streaming down my face. They coursed around to my nostrils and dribbled into my mouth. I had never cried so hard in my eleven years. I found the corner of the bed sheet and blew my nose on it. Still the tears gushed down in great relief. I was clean and pure, holy and sanctified. A copy of "Black Beauty" was on the bed beside me. I had just lived the life of a horse from its earliest days in the meadow with its wise mother and the pony Merrilegs to the fire in the stable, then the ruined knees incurred on a mercy gallop, to subsequently pulling a cabman's dray, and finally back to a meadow to live out life in retirement.

"Pauline!" A voice was calling me. "Come help me with dinner!"

How banal! After a spiritual experience such as I had just had, Mamma wanted me to go downstairs to set the table and mash the potatoes.

My own life was unremarkable. I lived in a predictable world of an intact family, meals on time with everyone there to eat together, lunches ready to be picked up by my father and us five children, clean clothes, and church on Sunday. There was nothing to write about, nothing to talk about.

But when I found "The Secret Garden" in a box of books the library had sent over to my seventh grade class, I was transported as a troubled child first to India then to England. I found a key that fit into the door in a wall of the estate owned by my guardian, and unlocking that door unlocked the pent up emotions of my young life, and I brought to bloom not only a garden but also a small boy whose legs had withered, not from disease, but from lack of use. I was a heroine.

In reality I lived in a house next door to the former mayor of the city. His estate took up a quarter of the block, and with his imposing large brick house and old maple tree on the side lawn, garages that had once been stables, a tennis court, I felt privileged to be a neighbor. I found he had his own secret outdoor area. It was close to our property. It was where they burned their trash. It was secluded and quiet. I liked to go into that area and sift through the ashes hoping to find the remnants of perhaps an old love letter. There wasn't much booty there, but I did scrape out of the earth an old locket. It had a picture of a young woman in it. A real treasure, I thought as I pocketed it.

And so it was through classic books that I became alive, vibrant. I read deep into the night, feeling that to go to sleep with a book unfinished was a small death. I became a half-breed when I read "Ramona," a beautiful young woman loved by the Spanish caballero of one side of her heritage, but loving and married to the full-blooded Indian man of her other side. I was wrenched to go through her trials with her chosen husband. I was outraged at the social injustice I was witness to and felt as if my own person had been violated. I got the same feeling when I read "Uncle Tom's Cabin," and I vowed I would never discriminate against anyone for color, race, or religion.

When I read "The Song of Bernadette," I was immersed in the past; I lived it; I was there. The past came into the present, and I realized that I had really lived a long time. Then the present went into the future, and it seemed I had an eternity on this planet.

In the late forties or early fifties "The Diary of Anne Frank" was published. Even though I knew it was a best-seller read by many, I felt like a snoop reading those pages of intimate thoughts of the little Jewish girl hiding out with her family in an annexe in Amsterdam. I could not put myself in her shoes. She was precocious. I was not. I was very ordinary, very attached to my mother, and I was inarticulate. How she was able to glean grist for the mill with her little stilted life was beyond my ability to comprehend then. But when I put the book down, I knew I had taken a journey – a journey many children had taken at that time, but a journey only one individual had given voice to.

And so I travelled in my youth on the magic carpets of books, living lives that were not mine, having family members not of my flesh, living in distant places like a child of a serviceman without ever leaving the comfort of my upstairs dormer room and the homemade bread and butter sandwich provided by my mother. Such spirituality I never captured in church or in religion classes. The flight on the wings of books enchanted me more than a flight on the wings of angels.

November 1, 2000

Consequences

What happens to a dream deferred
to yield to sensuous sirens,
to put off until another day
the education one needs for success?
I know. Although I avoided such,
I endeavor to help a friend who fell.
Eviction, hunger, unpaid bills
have been her lot in life.
She moans, she groans, she whines,
she cries.
Her life is boring, unfulfilled.
She sits alone in house all day
with children she bore that she cannot
bear.
Such is the fruit of untold passion
that does not consider consequences.

June 14, 2004

The House on Seneca Street

My father was orphaned at the age of four, and he and his two brothers were placed in a Catholic children's home. The good sisters there found them a patroness. She was a wealthy, elderly woman who had no children of her own. We knew her as "Auntie Val."

When Auntie Val died in 1938 or maybe 1939, she left a legacy of five thousand dollars to my parents. Back then that was a major fortune. My parents, unbeknownst to us children, went house hunting. One day before school my mother told me I was not to come back to the house, but that I was to go to 410 South Seneca. I knew the street. It was not far from where we lived. So after school I took a new route and walked to what would be my new home for close to fifteen years. I stood for a moment to take in the outside appearance of my new home.

I entered the house opening a front door which featured lead glass. On closing it I noticed a prism of colors dancing on the hardwood floor. "Ah!" I exclaimed as I looked into the living room. It was beautiful, elegant. A scrolled area rug covered the floor. New venetian blinds adorned the spacious windows and they were framed with drapes. A new plush sofa and chair of a maroon color were placed cattycorner opposite each other, and an occasional table with my mother's fish bowl on it shone in the light coming through the open slats of the blinds.

But what was this unattractive feature in an otherwise perfect setting? The old upright piano dominated a wall with a brigade of family pictures on its top as though we did not know what we looked like. Nevertheless, I was enchanted. Surely I must be "The Little Princess" who discovers her fine heritage.

Yes, this house was worthy of our aspirations to live as the well-to-do live, even though it was in the modest, low-income side of Wichita, Kansas.

September 22, 1999

The Last Goodbye

The natal home I was born into was comfortable, albeit modest. My parents gave me a feeling of security and constancy that engulfed any fears or trepidations I may have had. Three meals a day were as forthcoming as the light in the day and the dark of the night. Clean clothes were de rigueur as I trudged to school every day. It was sameness to the point of boredom, but it insulated me from the outside disasters of the times.

So, when I turned eighteen and had finished high school, I was reluctant to change my venue. I was as lodged in my place in my parents' home as a gumball becomes embedded in earth when stepped on after a rain. I did not have the courage to find a room somewhere or an apartment to be shared with another young woman as my own daughter did at that age. No. I commuted to the local university, and Mamma continued waking me up in the morning, preparing my breakfast, my lunch, and my dinner, and doing my laundry.

When I was twenty-five years old, I graduated from the university with a degree in Spanish and, a teacher's certificate. I needed a teaching position, and as it happened, there were none available in the city I called home; but two hundred miles away, in a little farming community, there was a need for a teacher with my credentials. I applied, interviewed, and I had a job. I found a furnished apartment to move into when I came up in the fall to fill my assignment. It was a part of the landlord and lady's house, and it had a bedroom, a big living room-dining room and a small kitchen. I would share the bathroom with the owners.

I spent the summer making an inventory of what I would take with me. Certainly my books (there were two fine bookcases in the apartment), the linens and bedspread and the electric blanket from my bed, the embroidered dresser scarves that I had made, knickknacks, and some pots, pans, dishes, and silver that Mamma culled from her stock. I borrowed $200 from my life insurance policy to pay for my first month's rent of $40, and for some groceries for me for the first month.

When the calendar was torn off to September, it was time for me to load up my Pontiac convertible and head to Spring Hill. It was my first venture away from home and family. My mother was not home the day I packed my car – she probably had a babysitting job. Daddy was there, and he very energetically carried boxes and clothes out to my car. He was exuberant,happy and relieved, I think, to see me finally getting out on my own. I kissed him “Goodbye”, got in the car and started it. Looking wistfully out the window, I waved a final goodbye. When I got out on the highway, my father's demeanor began to work on me. Was he really so glad to see me go? And my mother – hadn't this day warranted her staying at home and seeing me off? Did they care so little about me? The tears began to fall. Soon I could not see the highway. I pulled over to the shoulder of the road and sobbed.

“Can I help you, Miss?” I heard a male voice ask. I wiped my eyes and saw that it was a state trooper.

“No, no, it's nothing,” I blubbered. “I'm just leaving home

for the first time, and I feel a little emotional."

"Well, get a hold of yourself, Girl. I've been on my own since I was sixteen and glad of it. You have to toughen up."

I dried my eyes, thanked him, and started my car again. I turned on the radio and did not think again until I was in my apartment.

The awesome quiet of the evening spooked me. I had left two younger brothers and a younger sister at home, and there was always commotion there. This emptiness filled me with a longing for that which when I had it, I did not always appreciate.

I ate a solitary supper, spent a quiet evening puttering around, then went to bed and covered my head to ward off the feeling of loneliness and desolation and fear of the unknown.

It was several weeks and gains in friends and acquaintances and immersion in my work before I felt confident living alone. And never were my landlord and landlady aware of the fact that I settled in to think of them as my protectors against the night hoots.

March 23, 2004

Pauline Crowley

A Blossom Plucked

Mary Grace Sowers was a student of mine
Out on the Kansas plain.
Her family was wealthy, renowned, influential.
And Mary Grace benefited with smart plaid pleated
  skirts and cashmere sweater sets.
But her face bore testimony to a childhood polio bout.
The right side of her face
Frozen in a paralysed death.
The mouth on that side did not move,
And the eye was glass.

I had her in speech class,
Tremulous, frightened, shy.
She stood before the class.
In a falsetto voice and with body trembling
She delivered her speech.
Uncomfortable for her, I tensed and sweat,
But would not let her off the assignment.

One day I introduced a tape machine.
"Record a poem," I ordered,
"For to hear one's own voice
Is to master flaws."

Mary Grace improved, flourished, made friends.
And her father bought her a car.
Fine Plymouth station wagon, blue, sleek.
"She's driving too fast," whispered the mayor of the town.
"She's got to slow down," added the school principal.
"She's going to crash," murmured the merchants.
But no one admonished Mary Grace.

With a carful of friends,
She sped one day,
Down the highway of the state
And braked too fast for an intersection
  looming ahead.

Arms, legs, heads, torsos,
Tumbled together as the wagon
turned over and over.
And Mary Grace's glass eye
Went rolling down the road.
Symbolic of her death.

But life for the rest of us went on.
The next year's speech class sat in rows.
And the tape was introduced.
I snapped it on to "Play".
Clear, uninhibited, confident,
Came Mary Grace's voice.
  "When I am dead my dearest,
    Sing no sad songs for me."

But a tear rolled down my cheeks then,
And a tear rolls down today,
As I shoulder my guilt for not inculcating,
  "When you become a magnet,
  You have a responsibility."

January 17, 2001

Pauline Crowley

From There to Here

It takes some time
to appreciate how I once
forged a good mind
from a wrecked one.
How I won and achieved
wisdom and intelligence
from a quagmire of
youthful folly and faults.
I finally came to understand
that the novel is not
the only good reading written;
that the pop singers
aren't really as talented
as the classical singer;
that politics is more
than voting for a president;
that blindness to the outer world
affects my inner world;
that spirituality is not
necessarily a church thing;
that intelligence in more
than a 4.0 GPA average.

June 13, 2005

Betrayal

We wear the mask that grins and lies
about the pain and anguish we experience
when one so loved as our own dear son,
or husband, lover, significant-other
is faithless to his task of truth;
and honesty belies his acts
that hurt and hinder our own true love.
No longer free of the chains that bind
our consciousness to his deeds,
we feign at best ignorance, at worst indifference
to his cheating, sinful life
that nails us to a cross of wrath.

June 14, 2004

The Overworked Adolescent

As a teenager
I was compelled
By sense of neatness
To tidy the house.
I dusted, vacuumed,
Mopped, and picked up –
Oh! How I picked up
Every surface.
Books, magazines,
Jackets, material,
Games, scarves.

We were five kids,
Jean, Pauline, Bobby, Ruthie, and Joe,
(It sounds like a song title)
And my two parents.
There was barely enough
Room for us all,
Much less our stuff.

I hit on an idea
At the dinner table one eve.
I told the family I would put
Boxes on the back porch,

Label them,
    Daddy's dump,
    Jean's junk,
    Bobby's bunk,
    Ruthie's rubbish,
    Joe's jumble,
    And Mamma's miscellaneous.

My sister Jean
So quick-witted, so mean,
Quipped as I said
My last word:

"I suppose you will
Label your box,
Pauline's Precious Possessions."

August 14, 2006

Too Bad

Too bad
I can't
pump gas,
cut grass,
keep books,
compose
a song,
play ball,
cook peas,
read stats,
reap wheat,
guess beans,
jump rope,
leap frog,
cut smog,
drive fast.
I can,
thank God,
write poems.

June 20, 2001

A Dismal View

Memory fades, size diminishes.
Catch a glimpse, albeit obscure,
Mamma's youth, Oklahoma Prairie,
the last remnant of an old farmhouse,
once vibrant with life, with children.

The wellhouse gone, the washhouse gone,
Grandmother's cottage where hollyhocks grew
gone, no longer on the estate.
Gloom, murky now, a lone
old shoe at the doorstep
haunting the survivors who remember
a living farm complex.
Decaying wood on the once oft-painted
farmhouse a mute testament to disinterest –
disinterest of the heirs of the accoutrements
of a farm – a wheelbarrow, a shovel,
a stock tank, a pump.
Change happens, What was new
becomes old, and there is no
holding on to the present.

September 8, 2003

Pauline Crowley

When I Think of You

To the mother who knew
her bored child needed not new toys,
but a skill, a craft.
Embroidery, crochet, tatting,
You gave me all these talents,
and I have used them through the years.

Knowing what you, yourself, lacked,
you budgeted for my piano lessons,
my dancing, acrobatics, and singing.
I felt privileged beyond all wealth then –
And I still do.

The private school education
gleaned lifelong friends for me,
as well as knowledge not easily attained.

The clothes you sewed for me,
dresses, coats, and pajamas,
they fit so well and looked so good.

My manners, my openness,
I got it all from you.

Precious mother, gone now two years,
I hope I shone in your eyes,
Made you proud of me.
Lifted your spirits.
For you are yet alive
    in me.

December 9, 2002

Untitled

And so my grandmother, headstrong and wilful, mindless of her papa's wishes, embarked on a marriage sojourn that found her a pioneer woman in Wichita Falls, Texas, in a covered wagon. There she gave birth to my mother. Serena was educated and resourceful, but she was not above putting her shoulder to the plow to help her husband make a life for the little family. She collected scraps of material and made crazy quilts, feathering the pieces together, and sometimes embroidering the date or the state flower on a piece. She nestled in the wagon at night with her husband, Millard, and her baby, nursing the child as needed and also comforting Millard with that crazy quilt thrown over them to keep out the chill of the air.

When my mother was two or three years old, her father and mother made their way north into the Oklahoma Indian territory where the "Sooners" had recently claimed land on a run. They found a homestead a discouraged settler was willing to sell and left their domicile of a wagon to keep house in a little one-room structure which had never even been plastered.

Serena adapted to the difficult life there, and in the only letter we have that she wrote to her sister, she says, "Nell and I took the wagon out to the pasture today and collected a wagonful of dried cow chips. They will be splendid for heating the house in the upcoming winter."

She and Millard gave life to two more children, my uncles George and Dave. Serena sewed for the family. Without patterns she fashioned dresses, shirts, and night clothes with tucks, pleats, and puffs. Some of those clothes are still in existence. We have donated them to a woman who collects and shows vintage clothing.

She milked the cows, gathered the eggs, killed, cleaned, and fried chicken, and helped slaughter and preserve swine. The family was quite self-sufficient and she was up for the hard work and toil of running a farm.

It was not the rigors of her life that ended it but rather the poor medical practice on the prairie. She developed an ovarian cyst, and if the doctor had left it intact, it would probably have never bothered her, but he could not resist the impulse to lance it, as a teenager cannot resist the temptation to squeeze a pimple, and the infection spread. Millard took her to a hospital in Kansas City, but the damage was beyond cure, and she died at the age of thirty. She had been married fourteen years.

I sometimes wonder if my grandmother exists in me as I sit and sew. But could I kill and clean an animal? Perhaps if I had to, but the very thought is so distasteful to me that I think I would say "No" to a man who had nothing but a hard scrabble, scratch-it-from-the-earth life to offer me. I think Grandmother was capable of a love that has eluded me all my life. I have her genes, perhaps her wide-spaced teeth and her fine hair, but I am more inclined to follow the style of the woman who married Millard after her death – a woman who told her husband to mind the livestock and the garden for she had books to read and letters to write. The stepmother was the only grandmother I ever knew, and while I am sorry Serena died so young, I owe my existence to the events as they happened, and for that I am grateful.

Less is known about my father's mother, Lucy Borg. It is known that she was born in Switzerland and moved to Alsace Lorraine before coming to the United States. Lucy would have been familiar with mushrooms and made pâté, items unknown to the pioneers; she would have fixed quiche and cassoulet, clafoutis and soufflé. She spoke French, German, and English. She was intelligent, social, witty. And from her came the Catholics who now number to a hundred or so.

She too sewed, using lace as inserts, cut and tied threads, added tatting. She cared for the four children she gave birth to starting in 1900, followed in 1901, 1902, and the last child in 1903. She died young, also in her thirties, of tuberculosis. She left a deep void not only in her family but in the community.

Perhaps it was a tragedy that both of my grandmothers died so young, lamentable that not only I but their own children never knew them, but, my birth depended on it, as my mother's stepmother was a good friend of my father's benefactress, and through those two conduits my parents met and fell in love and formed a dynasty of their own.

The grandparents' blood has now been diffused with many new types, but every once in a while, in a great niece or nephew, I see spaces between the teeth that reassure me that my ancestors never really died.

May 14, 2001

Pauline Crowley

My Mother's Formal

I found it in her cedar chest
a week after she had died.
My mother's old cobalt blue formal.
The only one she ever had.
Lace, it is, with no other trim.
Simple, sensible – like herself,
Yet well-made by her own unwilling hands.
   (She hated formal occasions.)
The modest neck plunges to a V,
And there where her breasts
   would have met
   is a stain,
The mark of a cheap brooch.
The short sleeves have one small tuck
   for interest.
The skirt is flared –
   six-paneled
   three in front, three in back.
I inspected the hem.
It is narrow, fine stitching.
The formal is a size 16,
Huge, I thought at the time.
(I was a size 8.)
"I'll never let myself go like that."
I taunted Mamma.

Today I tried that formal on.
It fit me perfectly.

June 6, 2001

The Oklahoma Prairie

Spring will come to the Oklahoma prairie again,
And the yucca and the tumbleweed and the
buffalo grass will bloom.
The prairie birds will flit from telephone pole to
telephone pole.
But jackrabbits will only be seen in the memory
Of my generation that used to watch them
Race in front of a car.
The prairie dogs live now in a deep-fenced
compound at city park,
Having been burned out of their burrows
on the plains.
The bison only remain in the redskins'
Memory.
They are a part of the eternal dust that
swirls across the land,
Bedeviling the farmwives from Germany
or Scandinavia.

But spring will return again to the prairie,
And the yucca and the tumbleweed and
the buffalo grass will bloom.

September 6, 2001

Pauline Crowley

Once Within a Velvet Cocoon

Like hawks
we hunt our literary prey
with a sharp eye
a far-listening ear
and a gut-level wakefulness
to life's universe
of ever shifting shapes and sounds.
    But in the 50's
    we were apprentices
    testing our mettle.
    We met in the Alibi Room
    a coffee haven for
    stressed-out students.
    And we groped at intelligence.
    We listened to Thelonious Monk's jazz
    and we read the poems of Garcia Lorca.
        Our grasp of imagery
        was in its infancy.
        We smoked cigarettes around the rotunda
        and spoke Spanish.
        We made mobiles of
        the profound unity
        in our multifarious universe.
            We were in a velvet cocoon,
            wards yet of our parents
            yet away from their discipline.
            For us it was indeed the great get-away
            the golden age of reason and art.

May 25, 2004

1930

Nineteen-hundred-thirty bode bleakness across the country. An ominous financial depression had stolen the jobs of tens of thousands of men – family men who depended on an upswing economy to put bread on the table. And Mother Nature deemed it the propitious time to dry up the land then send winds across the plains to bedevil the farmers who also became hard pressed to put bread on the table – a bit of wild rabbit perhaps, but no garden produce.

No, it was no good time to bring squalling babies into the world, and I have no doubt a lot of back alley abortion doctors were kept busy, but we, the graduating class of 1948, were lucky. Our mothers not only gave birth to us, they loved us and wanted the best for us. They sacrificed to send us to Catholic schools. There, from our youngest years, we learned that God loves us and a host of other rather strict life ways that did not at the time impact on us. We were young, some from large families, happy, and lost in the romanticism of a good, Catholic life and the promise of happiness ever after (providing we follow the formula set forth by the Irish nuns.) The trappings of music and dance lessons, ice-skating, slumber parties and hikes sheltered us from the drudgery of our mothers' lives and the anxiety of our fathers to hold on to their jobs.

The Second World War caught us at age eleven clinging to our mothers, wondering what would become of us if America and the allies lost the war. We did our bit by buying victory stamps at school and writing to the men in service.

We entered Mt. Carmel high school when we were fourteen with some trepidation about whether or not we could do the work and be successful. But, once there, most of us found the work to be broken down into learnable parts, and we flourished. And we enjoyed the life there. Uniforms that were unsightly on individuals made an attractive line of chorus girls on their way to class.

We learned more about morals and virtues, good, clean living, and the tenets of the Catholic Church. To us, so young and inexperienced, they seemed easy to follow. We continued innocent, sweet, romantic, singing "The Things We Did Last Summer." Remember Tommy Bonhoff, Larry Chaney, Bob Ramer, Kenny Cornwall, Pinky What's his name?, the days and nights at Sandy Beach, Ken's Club, The Blue Moon, drive-ins? No, no one could touch us for the good, wholesome life of Mt. Carmel institute girls.

But, on graduation, we were welcomed into the real world. Some of us married right away, some of us went to the convent to become nuns, some of us to become nurses and teachers, but one thing was sure for us all. Taking care of ourselves was an ominous job as we had to make decisions that would affect us for life. Tarnished became the glow that had shone on us throughout school. We were ready for Vatican II when it came and the Women's movement in the sixties. We found new options – divorce, limiting the number of our children, careers.

Some of us took advantage of the open window through which we flew away from the strictures of the old life; others of us continued on the path that had formed us. But there was no hostility between the two groups. We were too small a constituency to sneer at each other. We needed one another for support, for comfort, for fun.

As our children left home and moved to the fringes of our lives, we started coming together again. Our own parents were aging and some of us were involved in their care. Then, to our horror, we began dying. How could a class of individuals once so young and vibrant start coming to the end of life? We were still too young with too much living to do – too immortal.

We gathered closer to each other – a remnant of a class that had not been large to begin with. There must be a bottle of wine, vintage 1930 or 1948, put away for the last survivor. But where is it?

Happily we still get together at frequent intervals and enjoy our avidness as of old. Perhaps in 2030 the last one of us who celebrates her one-hundredth birthday will clearly remember that day in May, 1948, when thirty-three girls dressed in white caps and gown marched into the blue chapel of the south wing of Mt. Carmel, received their diplomas, and sang for the last time, "Mother of Mt. Carmel, hear."

Up a Hill Slowly

He was my hero; she was my idol. We belonged to the same generation; we subscribed to the same religion; we had young children the same age. She was pregnant then in 1963, as was I. We both gave birth to boys in July, and we both named them Patrick. Her little Patrick died in infancy, and I had a severe postpartum depression that had me hospitalized.

John F. Kennedy was the epitome of action, of movement, of new ideas. His New Frontier policy gave aid to economically depressed areas in 1961. In March 1962, the major steel producers signed a contract with the steelworkers union that increased workers' benefits. And as for Civil Rights, Kennedy asked Congress to pass legislation requiring hotels, motels, and restaurants to admit customers regardless of race.

Oh! We of a Democratic bent were on a roll. Things were going our way. There was a lot of unrest, to be sure, especially in the South; but we knew it was time to change the entrenched ideas that Negroes were only good for manual labor and indiscriminate lynching and the workers were dispensable. It was time to bring all citizens into the main-stream.

Jackie Kennedy caught the fancy of the whole world. She was fashionable. Her hats were fetching. Her style of clothing was emulated throughout the country. She was so elegant, so intelligent – she spoke several languages fluently and she captured the admiration of the averse-to-anything-American French. She loved her children. They were the youngest to have inhabited the White House for a long, long time. No one knew of the dark secret Jackie bore of an unfaithful spouse.

And there I was: in a locked ward of a private psychiatric

hospital with a mind muddled and deranged, coping with the frightening electro-shock treatments. Would I ever be myself again? Would I ever be able to go back home? To take care of my children? To drive to the market? I was as much afraid as I was out of it.

Then it was November 22, 1963. The news reached us who were in the mental hospital that President Kennedy had been assassinated as he and his wife and his Vice President Lyndon B. Johnson drove through Dallas in a motorcade. Two or more shots rang out, and President Kennedy was hit in the neck and the head. He died.

We watched newsreels unfold on the big T.V. in the commons, hardly believing what we saw. To me it became a part of the phantasmagorias that swam and cavorted in my head. I could not separate reality from fantasy. What was real? Had I died – as I believed – and gone to a limbo waiting for judgment? Was this the end of the world? Who was this devil that came every day to fry my brain then quiz me about my past?

Jackie Kennedy and I were going to have to face new horizons – she, to cope with widowhood; I, to cope with a waffling mind. I could see the road ahead was long and arduous, but would it bring normalcy finally? Would the country survive the loss it sustained? Could we all get on with life? I was released after Christmas, and, with an animus yet trembling and a brain that felt bruised, I worked my way back into the household. The news became a blot – pushed out of my consciousness by the need to focus on the exigencies of my personal life. And what was Jackie doing? She was vacating the White House to what she hoped would be privacy and oblivion to her life and actions. But the press pushed hard and pursued her even as she walked down the street. For the rest of her life there would be not only tabloid accounts, but mainline newspaper stories of her comings and goings.

As for me, I went on a then new medication and worked to reclaim an independent position in life with no one suggesting any longer to me that I had been hurt in my childhood or that my sex life was not perfect; and if I would keep my mouth closed (and I usually do), no one would ever guess I have a bipolar disease.

Camelot is in the past – as if it had never existed. The characters are mostly gone: John, Jackie, John-John, Lyndon; but I, in my senescence, if asked, can still vividly recall the scene. But I have been through such a long, dark tunnel of my own that even to me those days are like a fairy tale.

October 15, 2003

Trinity, Illustration by Karen Gardner

Pauline Crowley

The Malignant Bellwether

if the strangling control
of the populace
by religion or by state
becomes a bellwether
for our actions
for our speech
for our belief
muffling our mouths
to echo only a leader
in whom we have
no credence

or chaining our hands
our feet
to conform to a standard
leaves us
slaves to righteousness
takes control from families
from individuals
from organizations
making hollow men
women, children
who cannot think
expand not minds
nor hear a drummer
of afar
nor think of solution
that would benefit

we are in trouble
we cannot cast off
the insidious
controls
that hinder our running free
free to think to learn
to discern to judge
to give abandon to inhibitions
to be ourselves

November 8, 2004

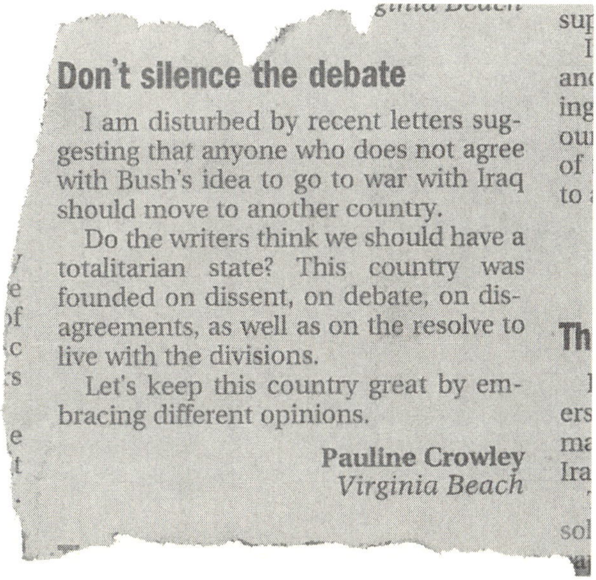

Don't silence the debate

I am disturbed by recent letters suggesting that anyone who does not agree with Bush's idea to go to war with Iraq should move to another country.

Do the writers think we should have a totalitarian state? This country was founded on dissent, on debate, on disagreements, as well as on the resolve to live with the divisions.

Let's keep this country great by embracing different opinions.

Pauline Crowley
Virginia Beach

A Narrative

A brave, bold soldier boy was I,
Sworn to defend or else to die
For an uncertain cause on the battlefield,
Not to give in, not to yield.
We searched and we searched for the enemy,
But we were not allowed to see
That the men facing us with explosives and guns
Were not the foe – were not the ones
We had to defeat. They were only the puppets
Of the awful regime of which we had heard snippets
Of news from the front.
And all that we had to confront
Exclude the ideology of the strange land
In which we found ourselves taking a stand.

We torched the child in the village.
We raped, we stole, we went on a pillage,
Our goodness, our honor swept away
by the madness, insanity that ruled the day.
I saw my comrades fall one by one
in a war that really could not be won.
I myself took a bullet in the shoulder.
You would not think such a wound would make me bolder.
But I advanced with an anger in my eye
and I pointed my weapon, and I let fly
a barrage of bullets which had no aim.
Like the miserable war with the miserable name.

Finally stateside I lived to see
a memorial built in Washington, D.C.
with the names of the fallen writ in stone.
I could not leave it alone. I could not leave it alone.
More of us died by our hand of suicide
than had fallen in the midst of the tide
that had swept us to our insanity.

Oh Lord! never again let it be.
I had to fight e'en to my death.
Let me stop here. I'm out of breath.

July 10, 2002

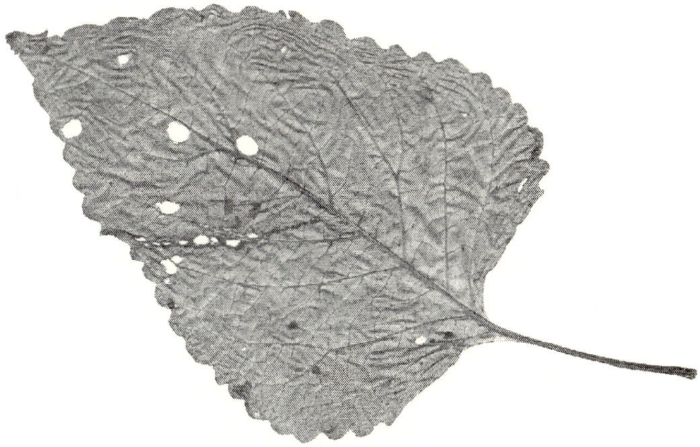

The ILL-TEMPERED Election Process

The race was on with far to go
Republicans and Democrats
They kicked, they squealed, they lied, they fought
Oh! What a ruckus they soon had wrought

Pundits bet and spread the news
No one was spared the worst of views
Of one side teeming hard against the other
A classic case of brother against brother

We hung together with our flock
And all the time the wicked clock
Kept ticking to an awful rhyme
Oh! We were having quite a time

With friends we took a different mien
And tried to show it did not matter
How we voted destroyed not our bond
We have good friends of whom we're fond

Life will go on no matter what
And winner will be pressed to cope
With budgets, war, and health care costs
And jobs without a decent wage

But underneath there fumed a fire
That our good man would quench the blaze
Of opposites who sought to win
No matter what the shape we're in

At last it's done, and we are free
To now relive the memory
And curse the other side until
We fight again in four swift years

October 15, 2004

The Folly of Deregulation

"The business of business is to make money,"
So declared the pundit.
But what if the market goes sour?
Then we want to know who done it.

"Laissez-faire needs to be in place.
Let the market make us wealthy."
But twice now in my lifetime,
Laissez-faire has been unhealthy.

The bookends of my life:
The 1930's depression,
And now that I am almost 80,
A shocking, debilitating recession.

When will mankind ever learn
That it doesn't pay to be greedy,
Because in the final analysis
That trait will make us needy.

January 20, 2009

In Your Own Best Interests

The frustrations of a world
With other people living in it
catapult the crazy to do crazy things
become benign when the people
write letters of reaching out
to the enemy. The master of the
art of harassment sends a dove
over the wall that separates him
from his object of derision And
children then walk to school in peace.
The local pub becomes a meeting place
and a draft is lifted in fellowship
with bones of contention falling away.
The powerful disburse their energy
into a holding catacomb where it can
do no harm. The wise share their skills
to the marginal minds so that they
themselves will be better served
when they are in a nursing home.
And everyone will find the world a
new womb where a halcyon comfort is known.

September 20, 2001

Pauline Crowley

Dreams in Our Hearts

We are born with dreams in our heart.
The toddlers in the nursery school
Ponder a day to come as the boy
pushes his truck, and the girl dresses her doll.
Let them be androgynous, is the cry of the day.
But each has his or her preferences
that belie the age they live in.

The elementary school child
who loves (or hates) his teacher
fosters new dreams for his days.
Perhaps to emulate; perhaps to go
beyond teacher's expectations.
They dream, but their dreams are muted
by realities all around them.

Perhaps in high school ambitions
will be resolved as strengths
show forth in disciplines.
One child aspires to be a builder,
another, the architect.
Dreams begin to jell,
a writer is here; a gymnast there.

But the watershed timed for dreams is college days
when hard decisions must be made
on careers, on marriage, and location.

On we go, dreaming even unto the end –
Will my writing ever be published?
Will my painting come to acclaim?
Will my students ever say, “She helped me”?
Will my policies endure?

Oh the fathers of our country
bequeathed to us the validity of dreams.
We need not idly daydream and despair
but work to make our dreams come true.
For we are born with dreams in our heart.

February 24, 2003

Pauline Crowley

Fuseli's Nightmare

It is rough terrain one stumbles over when confronted with an illness he or she must cope with for the rest of his life. The afflicted person goes through stages associated with dying – denial, bargaining, searching for a cure, and finally acceptance. It seems the younger the person, the more difficult it is to deal with the blow that rearranges the course of life unless, of course, the defect occurs at birth or infancy, when an individual knows no other status.

If I were to keep my mouth shut about my little impairment, and I usually do, so as to move more smoothly through the masses, obtain employment, be valued as a volunteer and such, no one would know that I suffer from a bipolar mental illness. At least, that is the most recent diagnosis, but when my mind waffles it is paranoia and delusions that plague me, not sudden euphoria followed by deep depression.

My mother must have noticed when I was very young that I was more volatile than her other children because she mentioned, before I was even ten, that "Pauline, you are like the little girl who had a curl right in the middle of her forehead, for when you are good you are very, very good, but when you are bad you are horrid." I remember the comment. I also remember I missed her point because I went to look in the mirror to see my curl on the forehead, and instead I saw a sober youngster with no curl but a lot of fringe that never grew long enough to do anything with at my temples.

I had two episodes of a near breakdown of my sanity before it finally blew when I was thirty-three. One was in the concluding days of a two-month trek through Europe which I took with my sister and my girlfriend when I was twenty. The other was a few years later when the high school boys I was trying to teach did not respect me and drove me to the brink of madness. The principal noticed my near collapse and talked to me. Thereafter I disassociated myself from my tormentors and did not engage in their banter and really ceased caring whether they learned anything or not.

But, in 1963, after the birth of our youngest son, life and chaos came crashing down on my fragile mental state, and I was hospitalized in Camelback Hospital, a private psychiatric institution in the affluent area of Scottsdale, Arizona. When the attending psychiatrist came in to assess me, I told him not to touch me – that my body belonged to God. Then I must have referred to him as the Devil, but I do not remember it. It came up later when I was out of the hospital and was seeing him on an outpatient basis. You see, my deluded mind told me I was dead.

My mind was very confused and pained me greatly. I wondered if I would ever be myself again. After the first electro-shock treatment, when my eyes were blurred from the treatment, I made my way down the hall to the great room where there were comfortable chairs and couches and a T.V. and magazines. But my eyes would not let me focus on the magazines and my mind precluded following T.V. A man came into the room whom I thought I recognized. He was my father's stature and size and his face resembled Daddy's, yet he was not Daddy, I knew. I decided it must be my Uncle Bill who had died when I was about eight years-old. I linked my arm through his and told him I was John's daughter. He asked me how John was and seemed to go along with my madness. He was as crazy as I was.

Thereafter I went through a haze and a maze trying to get my mental footing again. My will and independent spirit were gone; I was totally dependent on the doctor and hospital staff and my husband John. I could not speak on my behalf. On being discharged from the hospital three months after I entered it, I felt like a new person – but a very weak one. My sanity had been restored to me; although my mind felt bruised. When I mentioned it to my mother who had come to take care of my household and children while I was institutionalized, she assured me that my mind would get stronger and she gave me some scraps of corduroy to make a quilt of – therapy.

The visitations to the doctor in his office as an outpatient were gruelling for me. Actually, I liked dressing up and having a day out, and I did feel Dr. Beal had saved my life, but I was wary about talking to him. I knew from my father's tragic experience with a psychiatrist that one had to be careful what she said to a head doctor because they were trained to echo your words which could be very confusing if what you uttered was erroneous. The doctor's seeming agreement with you could harden your misconceptions, and your subsequent actions may not be in your best interest. So I skirted around the issues he brought up and asked when I could be discharged. He repeatedly told me I still had crazy ideas.

Over time he managed to work my poor little mind into a frenzy, and I lost myself. One night, when John was out of town on business, my head spun and raced and whirled. Even praying the rosary did not calm it down. I was in a panic. I put the kids to bed and went to bed myself but sleep would not come. I got out of bed and switched on the light and looked in the mirror to see if it were I looking back. Yes, it was, albeit my forehead was lined with the pressure. During the night I called the doctor's number. I got an answering service. I frantically told the woman who answered what I was going through, and she suggested I call a neighbor.

“Call a neighbour!” I wailed. “What could a neighbor do for me? I don't pay a neighbor to treat me.”

So she said she would get in touch with Dr. Beal. He called immediately. I told him about my frenzy, and he asked if I had any Librium. I had two pills. He told me to take both of them which I did and I was able to get to sleep. The next morning his secretary called and made an appointment for me to see him at the end of his day. I got a sitter and kept my appointment.

"You know," he confided in me, "when you called last night, I felt very sexual toward you. I thought, here is a frightened woman alone."

I could not believe my ears. I knew he had been trying to get me over my frigidity, but what kind of a doctor would make an admission such as his? And to such a desperate woman?

We were scheduled to move to California. I hoped I would get away from my madness there, but where I go, it goes, and without my medicine to keep me on course, I waffled again and had a three-week stay in another asylum. The doctor there was also a Freudian follower who believed all problems were related to sex and such past experiences, and I fled.

A third incident and I got a new doctor – a Jewish man who was intent on helping, not hurting me. He got me on a drug that is non-addictive and very effective and told me firmly to stay on it. He saw me every month for half a session for half the fee because I did not want to spend any time talking to him. Then, when John was scheduled to move to Virginia Beach, the doctor suggested I look for a mental health clinic which would reasonably monitor my medicine.

That is exactly what I did, and I have been very, very satisfied with it. My doctor changes from time to time as doctors retire or move on, but it matters not to me how competent the doctor is except at prescribing my medicine –

an elementary task that I could do myself. I have reconciled myself to my illness, but I do not know of any other person in my acquaintance who suffers such. There are many I know who have had breast cancer, as I have had, and many more who have high blood pressure and cholesterol and we commiserate together. None of my children are afflicted, and I have only one grandchild, so perhaps it will not be passed down the line.

I am no longer as myopic and introverted as I used to be, and my wide friendship and interest in others keeps me from dwelling on myself which leads to disillusionments and disorder. I feel strongly self-confident now and I don't think it will ever flee again.

My Mother - My Soul

Do you want to see my mother with her children?
Look at a Mary Cassatt painting.
The love, the care, the nurturing, the fondness
Hover in Cassatt's paintings as they did in my mother's eyes.
Her arms, so wonderfully strong
Lifted me out of a colony of ants
crawling up and stinging my legs.

My mother did not know how prescient she was
when she said to eight-year-old me,
"Pauline, you are like the little girl,
with a curl on her forehead.
When she was good, she was very, very good.
And when she was bad, she was horrid."

Then when I had the psychotic episode
And she hurried to my home to be caretaker,
My doctor intimated to me that
SHE was the basis of my mental illness.
A wanton maternal figure intent on submitting
me to her will and to her way – a childhood trauma.

How could I buy that? I was a disbeliever.
My head. My heart. My physical health.
This derangement was something awry in my chemistry.
Something that responded positively to Librium.
A daily dose – a mind on an even keel.

Mamma went unscathed, innocent as
She and I knew her to be. And once
again I viewed prints
painted by Cassatt in a bygone century,
And basked in the sunshine of my mother.

July 8, 2008

Winding Up in a Sheet

the first quarter turn
and foremost
we punch a clock
and not the least
nor yet the most
we render unto Caesar
a wedding band
forges a chain
that binds us to
fidelity
mortgages
diapers
tighter and tighter
we wind the shroud
Prometheus bound
that signifies death
to abandon to daydreams
but we love the prison
for it is our empire
to which we add daily
without impoverishing anyone
yet a hundredfold
enriching ourselves

April 28, 2003

The Dream

A mystic, mesmerizing miasma
Invades my sleeping space
Countless unimagined scenes revolve
I am young, virile, capable
Capable of teaching college students
Capable of soliciting door to door
From whence come such images?
Even in my vigorous youth
I was not so quite given to the success
I have at night in my subconscious
What would the head doctor say?
How would he analyze these dreams?
That they are wish fulfillments?
Or rejections of the truth?
These dreams are worth the sleeping
They give this feeble old girl life

The Elixir of Life

twixt the godly and the godless, the yin and the yang
the struggle for supremacy of Martha over Mary
I give homage to thee, oh JOY
I find you in the mundane, the cleaning of the house
the preparation of the meals, and in these
homely tasks, you are with me
but you are also there, oh Joy, when I play the part of Mary
and sit with the teacher learning new skills
discussing the complexities of life, meditating
is it this age at which I find myself
that you appear so prominently in my life
that at last there is time to enjoy
I only caught glimpses of your aura in the past
in schoolmarm days, in young motherhood

in the barren years between youth and old age
Be not fleeting but take off your hat
and stay for a long while

November 10, 2003

Tongue-Tied

There's something I want to say,
But the words will not come.
The thoughts get jumbled
up in my mind.
My audience sits and looks
and waits in anticipation.
They want to hear what
I have to say.
But the words will not come.
I need to collaborate –
collaborate with my mind
and get the important story out.
Others are waiting for my words.
But the words will not come.

Pauline Crowley

Sins and Omissions

"Maturity occurs
When one finishes her projects."
So spoke the good Home Economics teacher
When I was a girl.
But the message never got to my mother.
She has been dead six months now,
And I have finished for her
A Sunbonnet Sue coverlet that
She started on in nineteen-thirty-six
When she was expecting my little sister.
I have fashioned a tablecloth
Out of blocks embroidered with state flowers.
She worked them initially in nineteen-twenty-nine
When she was pregnant with my older sister.
I have made baby blankets,
Little dresses with bonnets and panties,
Blouses, skirts, sacques –
All from material she had purchased
With no thought in mind.
I recently pulled out a plastic box
And found in it polyester quilt blocks.
I hate polyester.
I cannot bear to finish them into quilts,
Nor yet can I bring myself to discard them.
What has Mamma done to me?

Locked me up in a tower, as Rapunzel
Or the Lady of Shallot, to work
The rest of my life on her unfinished
Business? Can't she see from where
She is that I have some ideas of my own?

October 4, 2001

Curls at Last

When hair becomes limp, stringy, and straight,
It needs a bit of help
  from the neighborhood beauty shop.
So thought my mother when
  I was five.

We entered a little shop on the corner,
I, holding my mother's hand,
  not fearful,
(that would occur the next time we came.)

I sat on a board put over
  the arms of the beautician's chair,
And she carefully, perfectly,
  cut my hair.
Then rolled it onto rods slim as a nail,
  All that went quite well.
But when she fastened
  metal clamps to the rods,
And the weight itself made
  my head feel heavy,
I knew I was in for something
  unpleasant.

Suddenly the heat on my head
  was unbearable.
A tear ran down my cheek.
I could not complain;
My mother had gone shopping.
Was that a scorch I smelled?
I tried to focus on the women
  who were having their hair waved,
Spit curls at the temples.
But my neck was burning.
When would this torture end?
At last the machine was turned off.
The rods were removed.
Curls, I had curls, oh so tight
  and frizzy.
The beautician combed them out
and set my hair in curlers.
Under the dryer I went.

When would the ordeal be over?

At last, my hair was finished
into Shirley Temple curls.
All over my head.
I looked so cute.
I was noticed at the fabric shop.
Had it all been worth it?
I wondered then, and

I wonder now.

January 10, 2001

Photo Property of Pauline Crowley

Pauline Crowley

d'Après T. S. Eliot

Lucy, oh Lucy, why did you soil your life
As a jeune fille soils her garments in the dirt?
You were so brilliant, so lovely, so scintillating
That all the rest of us felt shame for
Being so mundane, so profane.
Memory now being diminished,
I recall only that you spoke French fluently amazing
Others with your prowess also with numbers
And convoluted paragraphs anathema
To the common student.

Now to have come to this!
Disaster struck
When first you set eyes on Jordan.
Jordan, Jordan, Jordan.
I loved the name and the fine figure he cut,
But I noted a sinister gleam in his eye toward you. He
looked at me like that also, did you know?
His unfaithfulness did you in, created a
Shell out of a once viable creature, left
lusting after other women not once but twice
While you struggled with the ménage he abandoned.

Ah, my soeur, mon amie, mon idole –
How can I still be standing whenYou have fallen so far?

July 12, 2004

The Gardener's Girl

So you are the gardener's girl,
Dirty hands and leaf-strewn curl,
Muddy shoes and skirt awry,
Bruised knees, I wonder why.

Do you want to work as he,
In the outside air so free,
Digging in the mother earth,
Helping flowers and shrubs come to birth?

Noble work but simple tasks
As he keeps his tools in grasps
of hands that are calloused through and through.
Do you want to do that too?

Gentle girl of nature's best,
to toil and toil and only rest
at night time when you cannot see
the flowering beds around the tree.

We will give you accolades
As you work beneath the clouds.
We will hope for gentle rains
to bless your work along the lanes.

May 18, 2000

Untitled

A cat whines in the dark
Longing for its mistress
Who has gone to fair England
To be reunited with her husband

Her mother whines too
In harmony with the cat
Both feel the edge of despair
At having her gone

The cat carries in its mouth
A stick with a feather on it
Where is the mistress
Who used to play

The mother opens a hat box
full of seashells collected
Through the years
The scavenger of the beach is gone

So the cat sits on the mother's lap
A substitute for its owner
And the mother contemplates a new home
For the pet of her far-away daughter

January 13, 2003

Nostalgia

Gone are the May processions to Mary
Gone are the little flower girls who threw petals,
Gone are the maypoles around which we danced,
Gone are the ladies' sidesaddles of yore,
Gone are the bootblacks who shined our shoes,
Gone are the mothers who baked bread,
Gone are the windmills that pumped up water,
Gone are the bellboys who carried our luggage,
Gone are the curls of my husband's head,
Gone are the Gregorian chants at mass,
Gone are litanies which invoked saints,
Gone are the drugstore soda fountains,
Gone are the Five and Dime stores,
Gone are my precious poems of the distant past,
Gone are the generations that begat me, and soon
Gone are my peers and myself.

June 9, 2003

The Roar

All day the ocean was like regret,
Coming in, then fading out,
A churning of the mind that cannot rest
Because of an indiscretion in relationships
Or maybe in life decisions.
A gray day, to be sure,
Full of surges of misgivings that haunt
The otherwise quiet mind.
It does not rest; it does not shine.
It leaves tranquillity behind.
I cannot well undo the past.
But I can try to make amends.

January 26, 2004

Sleepless on the Night Train to St. Petersburg

Dusk was falling,
    barely lighting the way
    to the railroad station.
    We saw a man in the falling light
    Wrestling a woman with a suitcase.

"Walk on,"
our guide commanded.
"Stay close together."

A full moon presented itself
smaller in diameter in the East
than in our western hemisphere.

Eerie, it was, there in the Moscow station.
The Russian language augmented
the darkness that fell,
and I thought of Tolstoy, or
Pushkin, or Pasternak.

Shades of Dr. Zhivago.
Was I in a movie?
An actress in a scene
on a made-up set?

We found our compartment,
two to a room
a bunk on each side.

"Here, jam this in your door!"
and a large dowel was thrust at us.
It was to keep intruders out.
How comforting!

Pauline Crowley

I tried to sleep
but the window - the window
beckoned me to peep out.
Birches with their white trunks,
gleamed in the moonlight,
casting darkness on the snow.

We stopped,
a village appeared
as if in a fairytale
little cottages, wooden fences.

On we went,
I saw a bear
newly out of hibernation,
too early, too early.

It was cold outside,
frosty and cold.
But still.
So still.
Eternally still.

November 25, 2002

Courting Sleep

Float on a cloud, drift on a breeze,

Compose a poem; count sheep.
Oh sleep, come and steal my
    consciousness away.

I think I saw an image, a dream –

But now it has eluded me.

I am awake.

How do I turn this motor off?

How do I let go?

The day passes in review; tomorrow is a preview.

Should I arise and quit this charade?

No. Wait! I can now focus on a light. It pulls,
    it beckons, it...

November 29, 2000

Pauline Crowley

Ode to Coffee

Oh sip, oh slurp of heavenly brew,
Of lowly beginning I shall relate,
You warm the frozen, sober the inebriated,
Awaken the slumberer, quicken the slow.
How humble I feel at your power.

Oh to the goats which gamboled in Ethiopia
So many centuries ago,
And ate of the bean of an unnamed bush.
The shepherds who noticed the active wakefulness
Of the animals through the night, said
"Let us keep the goats from the accursed bush
But brew ourselves a drink."
So coffee was introduced into the world.

Oh to Pope Clement VII who stated,
"Who said coffee is a drink only for infidels?
Bring me a cup of that black beverage."
Thereafter the Christian world established
The popular coffeehouses so well attended.

Oh, to the conferences, confidentialities, contracts, convivialities
That come to heads over cups of coffee.
Long live the ancient drink without which
Today's household could not exist.

May 29, 2002

Dreams Deferred

I've known an edginess come evening
A presentiment that never came to fruition.
What I have in my hand does not glitter.
I covet the Will-o-the-wisp gleaming afar,
It is whimsy, illusive, unreachable.
I hesitate between the things that help
And the things that hurt.
The theme I write so eloquently
At night in my head, my dreams, my imagination
Alas, turns to trash when I recollect it on paper.
The words crumble around me and drop
Like leaves to the ground.
I feel trapped between the fire and the flood
Unable to soar to literary heights
Hobbled by my inadequacies,
Envious of other writers, so mystic.
I live and breathe longing for that writer's fame
That time juggles and dissolves into lies and cheats.
That facet of my life that I would treasure
Becomes a shard shattered on concrete.

November 28, 2006

United

I

The ever loving, willing wife
who forbears any crisis

YOU

My man exceptional and wise
stands ever with me.

SHE

The talent of the filial knot
that binds us as ken

THEY

The boys who made us lose our cool
Now subject to God

WE

The family against the grim
triumphed over all

November 14, 2005

Mighty Pain

A mighty pain it is to love too much.
And 'tis a pain that pain to miss for'ere.
But of all pains the greatest pain, no doubt,
It is to love in vain another's treasure.
The star-struck lovers envied by their peers
Are oft to feel a pang of quick remorse
On finding they have wounded loved one's hearts,
And grieve for torment they themselves have caused.
But quick to say "forgive" they mend their ways,
And hope to live with only rendering
Their lives and souls to each his own true love.
Alas, too often parting on a bitter note
Is fate of couples smitten by the arrow.
Forgive me if I now resort to sorrow.

June 13, 2001

Pauline Crowley

The Ubiquitous Apron

It is an atavistic thing with me – a throw-back to earlier generations of my womenfolk. It is also a hallmark of our station in life – that of a working woman, either as a woman on a farm doing not only the inside labor of cooking, laundry, and child-care, but also outdoor chores such as milking cows and gathering eggs; or as the maid, cook, or laundress in a city family. That was the ilk into which I was born – a long line of apron-clad women.

I remember the women of my mother's generation – women who were homebodies charged with the care of the house and cooking as well as the gardening and the chicken raising and killing, cleaning and plucking before being put into the pot. They all donned an apron first thing in the morning, not one of those that started at the waist and was held with a tie behind the body, but one with a bib. And they were always, always ones that went over the shoulders.

One day my mother had my older sister Jean and my younger brother Bobby and me stay on the back porch while she disappeared into the chicken coop to get us a "surprise". She came back holding up the skirt of her apron, and, when she reached us, she put her free hand into that apron and pulled out a little, yellow, baby chick for each of us. That speaks for the magic of aprons.

So, naturally, when I announced my engagement to be married to John, my mother presented me with an apron she had made. Ironically it had no bib; it was an apron gathered on a waist band that tied behind. A small towel had been gathered and sewn into the band – handy for quick wipes. It was a lady's apron. I rebelled at that time – against the whole patriarchal society that landlocked its women into the untenable role of a lifetime of near slavery what with cooking, cleaning, and rearing children being our lot. I wanted that scene, to be sure, but I wanted more – a life away from the apron. It was the first dawning of the Great Women's Liberation Movement, and I was at its forefront.

But the weight of the family history was not easily discarded. For one thing I found I enjoyed cooking and was willing to tackle all sorts of recipes. John's salary covered pricy ingredients and flops – BUT, if I did not wear my apron, the flour would powder my skirt or pants and sauce would take care of my bodice.

I graduated then into the full body apron, using the one my mother had made me when company came. Those aprons served me well through the years, but I was always glad for a day to get out of them and meet with my girl friends for bridge or lunch; later I was a substitute teacher and was happy for another day of stimulation. I half envied those women such as my sister Jean who had full time jobs, but deep down I knew if I had a full time job, I would be longing for my free days at home wearing my "necessity" – the apron.

"Tied to her apron strings" was an old adage we used to refer to children, usually a young male, who could not separate from his/her mother. Well, I was tied to the apron strings not so much of my mother as to my chosen station in life, and I have by now well adjusted to being its prisoner.

March 9, 2004

Pauline Crowley

Coming to Terms with Love

Plural has been the celestial history of my heart.

Elmer was flattering, seductive, attractive.
He whispered how he loved me, how only I
had what he wanted.
But I sensed a will to control, to snuff creativity,
to hinder knowledge, to kill initiative,
And I escaped with a shrug of my shoulders –
Not to look back.

Bernard was foreign, a torch in the dark
to light my beleaguered way.
And I would have surrendered had he
not sensed my trap and absconded
with my heart.
Oh woe!

Leo was a likely match for myself
As I passed the quarter century age.
Well employed, religious, up to date,
A dancer of the first water.
But his close scrutiny of faults
of everyone, including me,
Led us onto separate paths –
Albeit a pang of longing followed him.

Dare I say I loved them all?
For love's sweet knowledge escapes my ken.
And the lust in chemistry muddies the water.
But trust in alterations to fit a mold
led one to conjugal happiness.
And if love be abandoned to good sense,
Then something feeling like love ensues.

January 17, 2002

Ode to John

He came into my life, all glitters and gleams,
Good old John from New Orleans.

I knew in an instant that he was the man of my dreams,
Good old John from New Orleans.

I won him with plots and sometimes with schemes,
Good old John from New Orleans.

And we wed in the season of cake and ice creams,
I and my man from New Orleans.

Then he went off to work with computers and teams,
Good old John from New Orleans.

He brought home the money in envelopes, then in reams,
Best old man from New Orleans.

He gave me three children who pulled at my seams,
Good old John from New Orleans.

We raised them through childhood and then through their teens,
Big bad dad from New Orleans.

And then he retired, and I had the screams,
Good old John from New Orleans.

I guess we'll go on forever it seems.
I and my darling from New Orleans.

Tug of War

She was the seductress; he, the seductor,
But their dreams were opposite: hers, the altar; his, the bed
As they struggled together on the dining room floor.

He desired a quick orgasm; she wanted more.
He wanted to score and be gone; she, to wed.
She believed him a knight; he, her a whore.

They felt their ambitions rise, float, and soar,
But each had ideas of what lay ahead,
She, the seductress; he, the seductor.

She kept her knees tight and he thought he tore
The ribbon that held her tresses to her head.
But it was only the dog's bow that he bore.

Then suddenly he knew as if he felt a roar
That the mind of the girl could now be read.
He wanted drama; she wanted lore.

She wouldn't follow, and he wouldn't be led.
They saw clearly that separation was their fate instead.
She resisted and shivered and showed him the door;
She the seductress; he the seductor.

March 10, 2003

The Life of Love

Like the everlasting tide, love ebbs and flows
changes eternally as the water in the river
From infantile affection for a mother
to a surge of hormones for a young couple
of pubescence. Then enchanted newlywed
lovers cozily ensconced in a secret nest
of their first apartment – the TV, the computer,
the Blackberry turned off affording privacy.

Some time later the inconvenience of a lustful crush
for a doctor, a co-worker, a pastor: nemesis of
fidelity, witness to the evanescence of conjugal love
that threatens to unravel the fabric of stability, even
though the desire be unfulfilled. Hopefully, good
sense prevails and the spouse looks good again.
Grateful for the forbearance, love sparks abloom
with kisses, backrubs, smiles, and gratitude.

Each moment has its place
in the flow of time, and if you
reach back for it, it becomes a
handful of dust.

Longings of the Heart

What thrills my soul
Is not mundane, nor trivial,
Nor facile to adhere to.
It is the nebulous belief
That I am more than
What I see.

Save me from a stupid life
I pleaded with my teachers
In my youth.
It's not the way I look
Or sing a song.
It is the words I write –
The thoughts I think
That separate me from the others.

I don't always pursue an idea.
But velleity does not
Fulfill my innermost desires.
I must be active to attain my dream.
Something as ordinary
As a poem
Can extend my life,
Give me immortality.
For the heart has reasons
Which reason cannot understand.*

* Blaise Pascal

People Will Say

When I was young
and my face was breaking out
and my heart broke
when Larry said, "It's over."
When I was rebelling against Mamma,
and the teachers did not understand me,
and my older sister bossed me,
and I lamented my lost tomboyishness;
when chores and homework assailed me,
and I longed to have a job but would not look for one,
and my sexuality tormented me,
and I complained bitterly,
        they said,
  "Get a life – get a life."

When I reached middle age
and my waist thickened,
and my children rebelled;
when no one would listen,
and depression set in,
and I needed a new car,
and I couldn't keep up the house,
and I lost my identity
        I heard
  "This is the first day of the rest of your life."

Now that I am old,
and I color the gray,
and I tolerate the wrinkles,
and I rejoice in the morning
because I have awakened,
and I walk in the dew barefoot,
and I seek young companions,
and I slide on the ice,
and I read the cartoons,
    the word is,
  "Act your age."

May 12, 2003

Holy Grail

I keep a blue bottle
reminiscent of romance
exotic vessel
purveyor of spirits

long lost times
happiness unparalleled
passionate love
toasts to eternity

flower holder now
mellow with age
cobalt, vermillion, scarlet
sparklers in the sunlight

a testimony to life
drunk to the fullest
unbroken through years
and heirloom for the future

April 11, 2005

Regrets

I stand in
the courtroom
of conscience
a mighty
judge it is
transgressions
of times past
haunt me to
imprison
my weak mind
doomed to guilt
free me now
from fear of
just revenge
and let my
old age soon
be at peace

The Noiseless Moment

Alone in the house in my rocking chair
        I sit

No sound in there to stir my feathered nerves
        no noise

No husband to command my attention
        no TV

No birds outside to catch my ear
        no twittering

I muse and contemplate and think
        my habit

And bless this day when I can recollect

May 9, 2005

Ode to Death

Death, you have stalked my DNA through my genetic
ancestors throughout the centuries.
I evaded you in prehistoric times and I will keep
you at bay as I go into my senescence.
You tried to claim me during the Christian persecutions,
then during the Black Plague your noxious presence hovered around my kin.
But like Wiley the Fox I keep emerging to
claim my place through the ages.
Most recently you lingered at the operation table
when I had a malignant tumor removed from my breast.
And I saw you lurking at the bedside when I was
eighteen and had a severe case of scarlet fever.
But I keep on dodging cars and mosquitoes
and ill-fated planes and boats, and you can
just sit there ignobly hoping for your final triumph.
But when you do come, you will be bearing a feast
of red meat, eggs, cheese, cream, butter, and alcohol.

So Death, be not proud, for in the end you are really
only the servant of all things.

March 25, 2003

Jumpin' Jehosaphat!

I was cleaning up my deck the day after Isabel when I uncovered a frog — a full-grown, adult frog. I was so happy to see the little fellow, I could have kissed him, but I was afraid he would turn into a prince. And frogs are more beneficial to the environment than princes.

There used to be a plethora of frogs in our area, but this is the first one I have seen for years. Long live frogs!

Pauline Crowley
Virginia Beach

Virginan-Pilot, September 28, 2003

Index of First Lines

New, young teachers can't know everything

Too much knowledge is expected of new teachers fresh from college.

I took the National Teachers Examination 10 years ago to become certified. I passed with a wide margin, but I must admit I was already 60 years old. I had lived through much of the history that was on the test, and I had helped my own children learn history that predated me.

I had had leisure time to read encyclopedias. I had worked in insurance, rating policies and figuring my salary when I was on commission.

I had made drapes and curtains and quilts, figuring how much material was needed. I had been a member of a great books discussion group. I had paid bills.

Does the administration think we learn everything we're ever going to know in the few years we spend in school? To be sure, every teacher should be able to read and reason. But many coaches and instructors of music and dance have students who outperform them. That does not take away the skill of the instructors.

I say give every literate would-be teacher the right to try his or her hand in the classroom, and make sure there are teachers' manuals for math.

Pauline Crowley
Virginia Beach

■

Virginian-Pilot, May 24, 2001